IMAGES
of America

MIDDLETOWN'S
HIGH STREET AND
WESLEYAN UNIVERSITY

On the road to Middletown from Hartford, a 19th-century traveler would descend Prospect Hill and pass a row of 50 Lombardy poplars, enjoying a panoramic view of the Connecticut River valley below. In this view of 1836, Chatham's Gildersleeve shipyard is to the left beyond the village of Cromwell. Three miles away is Middletown rising from the shores of the meandering river, its church spires delineating its Main Street and, to their right, the buildings of the town's new Wesleyan University crowning High Street. From this vantage point in 1771, Pres. John Adams, who had visited many New England villages, said, "Middletown, I think, is the most beautiful of all." (Middlesex County Historical Society.)

ON THE COVER: Coeducation came to Wesleyan University on High Street in 1872. In 1889, Wesleyan purchased the Heth Camp House (left) for female students, then called Webb Hall. Although they typically excelled academically, by 1892, only 43 women had achieved graduation. The women established sororities and even a baseball team of their own. The "college ladies" were nicknamed "quails" by their campus brothers, and Webb Hall became known as the "Quail Roost." (Wesleyan University Library, Special Collection & Archives.)

IMAGES
of America

MIDDLETOWN'S
HIGH STREET AND
WESLEYAN UNIVERSITY

Alain Munkittrick and Deborah Shapiro

ARCADIA
PUBLISHING

Copyright © 2020 by Alain Munkittrick and Deborah Shapiro
ISBN 978-1-4671-0546-0

Published by Arcadia Publishing
Charleston, South Carolina

Printed in the United States of America

Library of Congress Control Number: 2020933865

For all general information, please contact Arcadia Publishing:
Telephone 843-853-2070
Fax 843-853-0044
E-mail sales@arcadiapublishing.com
For customer service and orders:
Toll-Free 1-888-313-2665

Visit us on the Internet at www.arcadiapublishing.com

*The authors dedicate this book to the archivists,
cataloguers, and students of Middletown's history who
preserve our heritage for tomorrow's scholars.*

CONTENTS

ACKNOWLEDGMENTS

Most of the images selected for this book appear courtesy of the Wesleyan University Library Special Collections & Archives (WULSCA) and the Middlesex County Historical Society (MCHS). For their invaluable assistance, we thank Suzy Taraba, Amanda Nelson and the staff of the WULSCA, and Maria Weinberger, executive director of the MCHS.

The following people and organizations also provided images: Alain Munkittrick (AM); Beinecke Rare Book and Manuscript Library, James Weldon Johnson Collection, Yale University (BRBML); Connecticut Historical Society, gift of Dr. William J. Russell (CHS); Colonial Williamsburg Foundation/Hollins University (CWF/HU); Davison Art Center, Wesleyan University (DAC); John Giammateo Photographs (JG); Library of Congress, Prints & Photographs Division (LC); Metropolitan Museum of Art (MMA); Middletown Russell Library (MRL); US National Archives & Record Administration (NARA); New Haven Museum Photo Archives (NHM); Sullivan Museum & History Center, Norwich University (SMNU); Shining Hope for Communities (SHOFCO); University of Maryland Libraries, Special Collections & University Archives (UMD); Clive Connor; Jill Hunting; Stephen J. Roper; Samuel Russell; Josephine Saraceno Vassallo; the family of John Colton Wells III; and Katrina Winfield-Howard.

We are grateful for the assistance we received from Denise Mackey-Russo, reference librarian at Middletown Russell Library; photographer John Giammatteo; Cassandra Day, Hearst Media Connecticut; Katherine Taylor-McBroom, curator of exhibits and collections at the Sullivan Museum & History Center of Norwich University; Miya Tokumitsu, curator of Wesleyan University's Davison Art Center; Molly Frank, development associate at SHOFCO; Angela Moore, Beinecke Rare Book and Manuscript Library; Jason Bischoff-Wurstle, New Haven Museum; Olivia Drake, Wesleyan University; Billy Faires, Hollins University; and Owen Panettieri, 5000 Broadway Productions.

Others who helped the authors in many ways include Craig Ashley, Susan Brooks, John Fletcher Bolles, Denise Desplaines, James Dresser, Jack Gorlin, Jane Harris, Robert Hubbard, Joyce Kirkpatrick, Leith Johnson, Elizabeth McAllister, Rosemary Munkittrick, David Mylchreest, William Pinch, Karl Harrington Potter, Karl Scheibe, Sarah Shapiro, Suzanne Shapiro, and Carol Wells.

We also wish to thank Erin Vosgien and Angel Prohaska with Arcadia Publishing for their invaluable guidance throughout this project.

Introduction

Life in Middletown at its founding in 1650 centered around the meetinghouse built in the middle of Main Street on a small rise above the Connecticut River. Farming was the primary occupation of the first settlers who arrived from the Hartford area and Massachusetts Bay Colony, but it was soon discovered that the river could provide a deepwater anchorage, facilitating greater maritime activity. Locals claimed a stake in the West Indies trade, shipping Connecticut agricultural produce and horses to Caribbean islands in return for sugar, molasses, and rum. Regrettably, enslaved people were also imported. The West Indies trade made Middletown the largest town in Connecticut in the mid-18th century and supported new industry, especially artisan pewter makers whose products rivaled those of Boston and Philadelphia. The merchants and sea captains became wealthy, building their homes between the unusually wide Main Street and their wharves on the river.

As steamboats and railroads replaced sailing ships for commercial trade, Middletown residents turned toward manufacturing to sustain the local economy. Samuel Russell, originally a China trader in goods such as tea, porcelain, silks, and opium, founded the Russell Manufacturing Company, which produced suspenders and other woven products. Nathan Starr, Nathan Starr Jr., Simeon North, and others produced swords and various firearms, including muskets, rifles, and pistols. William Walter Wilcox partnered with Albert Crittenden to manufacture marine hardware, and the Hubbard brothers, Gaston and Samuel, ran a thriving lumberyard on the riverbank. A number of woolen mills were established, and W&B Douglas Company shipped its hydraulic pumps throughout the world.

This manufacturing in Middletown was aided by waterpower supplied by local tributaries of the Connecticut River, such as the West River, Pameacha River, Sanseer Brook, and Sumner Creek. Dams were erected on these waterways to harness the power, and some are still in existence, notably the one at the Starr Mill complex, still in use today. The woolen mill established by Alexander Wolcott and Arthur Magill in 1810 was possibly the first steam-powered factory in the nation.

Middletown's captains of industry sought to live apart from their places of business and eyed the tall hill above the river that had attracted earlier settlers. Those first houses on the hill were spare in design, constructed of wood and stone. Farmers and notable residents, such as early Congregational ministers, typically erected center-chimney clapboard structures for their homes. Rev. Noadiah Russell, who was called to be the second pastor of the local church in 1687, built his family homestead on the crest of the hill that became High Street, as did Rev. Enoch Huntington, who served the church from 1762 until his death in 1809. Private schools for younger students, such as those operated by Isaac Webb, Rev. Henry Colton, Georgianna Minor, and Elizabeth and Anne Patten, were later established in homes. The street's association with education continued with the 1831 founding of Wesleyan University, which occupied Capt. Alden Partridge's American Literary, Scientific, and Military Academy's buildings when it moved from Middletown.

Known for its spectacular views of the river's great bend from its high elevation, the street was officially named in an ordinance passed by the Court of Common Council on July 5, 1809:

"The Highway from Washington Street at the N.W. corner of the late Col. Hamlin's home lot to Warwick's bridge shall be called High Street." Fortunately, plenty of vacant land remained for the rising industrialists' lofty residential visions. The Russell family acquired the entire block bounded by High, Washington, Pearl, and Court Streets that originally included the family homestead, and Samuel Russell erected his grand Greek Revival villa. His brother Edward Augustus Russell razed the Rev. Noadiah Russell homestead of his ancestors to build his own fashionable home. The families of other industrialists such as the Starrs, Hubbards, and Wilcoxes either built on vacant land, demolished, or moved homes to other streets to claim perfect sites for their new residences. One after another, these families built stately homes, many of which survive today. Most are now owned by Wesleyan University, but some are still lovingly cared for by private citizens.

Manufacturing continued well into the 20th century in Middletown, attracting immigrant labor from Ireland, Sweden, Poland, and Italy. In 1936, a massive flood of the Connecticut River and a strike at the Remington Rand Corporation (typewriter manufacturers) affected the town's economy. Many companies, originally run by their founding families, were either closed or acquired by outside corporations, causing many of the elite owners of homes on High Street to seek residence elsewhere. In addition, the cost of maintaining these palatial homes proved to be too exorbitant for these families in their reduced circumstances, and they donated or sold them to an expanding Wesleyan University.

Wesleyan University repurposed these grand homes and other buildings it acquired on High Street for academic uses, while razing some to make room for more modern construction. The Greater Middletown Preservation Trust, formed in 1972 to save the city's South Green, became an active voice to save the colonial and premodern character of High Street. Five structures, the Coite-Hubbard House, the Edward Augustus Russell House, the Xi Chapter Psi Upsilon fraternity house, the Richard Alsop IV House, and the Samuel Russell House, have been listed in the National Register of Historic Places. The latter two have also received prestigious national historic landmark status. For many years, the Wesleyan Landmarks Advisory Board, composed of faculty, alumni, and students, also advised the university on adaptive reuse of its historic buildings.

With academic buildings, arts venues, and resources like the college health center, High Street continues to be the center of campus life for Wesleyan University. When school is in session, students and faculty crisscross the quadrangle in front of College Row in a rush to get to classes or set out for the walk down the hill to the shops and restaurants lining Main Street. Farther south is a day care facility in one of the colonial houses where faculty children can be heard playing. Stoplights at crosswalks modulate a steady flow of automobiles on the street that once was traversed by horse-drawn carts and carriages.

At the time of the birth of the Republic, George Washington came to High Street. Later visitors such as Ralph Waldo Emerson, William Howard Taft, Richard Nixon, Rev. Dr. Martin Luther King Jr., and Barack Obama enjoyed enthusiastic welcomes. Many professors who lived on High Street and scholars who visited have been leaders in their fields of study. Countless graduates from all over the world have spent their formative years on High Street, and many return every year for commencement and reunions.

High Street is inextricably linked to the history and life of Middletown and reflects the nation's journey from trade and industrial development toward an economy based on knowledge. The buildings on the street advanced the aesthetics and aspirations of the day, and the people who lived here shaped, and still shape, our community through their leadership in business, academia, and politics. Through the passing centuries, a stroll down High Street has always been, and today remains, a treat for the senses and the intellect.

One

HIGH STREET:
"PARADISE ROW"

The ridge of land 175 feet above the Connecticut River formed a natural plateau that would be High Street's seat and Middletown's most desirable address. Vernon (later Foss) Hill gently rose to its west, beyond which Indian Hill formed a dramatic backdrop. This plateau provided a vantage from which to enjoy panoramic views over the town and harbor below. Visible beyond was the graceful arc of the river leading to the dramatic, narrowing straits and Fort Hill to the south. Across the river to the east were the Chatham (now Portland) brownstone quarries with Great Hill in the distance. Diarists, reporters, and property advertisements acclaimed these views. Fiction stories with settings modeled after High Street described them in purple prose. Visitors touring High Street recorded their lasting impressions. George Washington, on a brief stop in 1789, wrote simply, "I took a walk around the town from the heights of which the prospect is beautiful."

High Street residents recognized their special setting. Before zoning regulations, they added restrictions to deeds of land preserving their views. Some insisted on home setbacks from the street to encourage more space for plantings to be enjoyed by all. It paid off. By 1855, one reporter wrote, "The tall overarching elms and the handsome grounds adjoining the walks on either side, make a stroll or a ride through it [High Street] one of the luxuries of the season."

High Street was embellished with a variety of green spaces: an early pleasure garden, a town green, a campus quadrangle, and a naturally wild ramble. These green spaces were linked by rows of elms, oaks, and maple trees that bordered expansive lawns enhanced by garden beds and specimen trees. Contemporaneous with the development of New Haven's Hillhouse Avenue and Asylum Street above Hartford, High Street residents and their designers similarly crafted a parklike neighborhood. Such special districts reflected the 19th century's Romantic period when London's Regency–Era parks, studded with compact villas, became the model for imitation here. This early suburban model, or rus in urbe (country in city) resulted in High Street, Middletown's "Paradise Row."

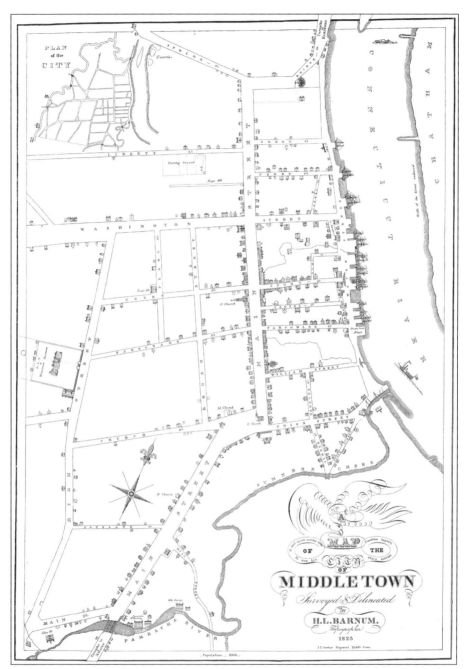

H.L. Barnum, a cadet at the American Literary, Scientific, and Military Academy on High Street, drew this map of Middletown in 1825. His academy (center left) dominated the sparsely settled High Street at the west side of the growing town. Streets that led up to High Street from the wharves along Water Street were named (north to south) Washington, Court, Parsonage, Church, and Loveland. William Street (between Parsonage and Church Streets) came soon thereafter. Washington Street headed west toward Meriden. At its south end, High Street merged with a leg of Main Street (now Warwick Street) that crossed the Pameacha River to Trench Hill, where Highland Avenue now commences. That road took travelers to Durham and New Haven. (MCHS.)

10

Early painted views of Middletown from the Chatham side of the river depict High Street on the highest ridge of land running north to south parallel with, and about three wide blocks above, the Connecticut River. The c. 1798 view above was painted by a daughter of the Birmingham, England, merchant and important proponent of Unitarianism William Russell. She depicted High Street with four houses, barns, and the Congregationalist's First Church at its south end (left of center). By 1845, Main Street, with its three churches and courthouse, depicted below, was the commercial center of Middletown. The nascent Wesleyan University's large buildings dominate High Street, but the columned Samuel Russell house (upper right) and other more fashionable homes have made their appearance at the top of the hill. (Above, CHS; below, AM.)

11

By 1877, when Oakley Hoopes Bailey made his bird's-eye view of Middletown, High Street was—after Main Street, which paralleled the riverfront—the most prominent south-to-north (left-to-right) artery. Twenty of the city's finest mansions lined High Street, which stretched from the natural cleft in the landscape called Pike's Ravine (upper left) to the long, rectangular Washington Park (upper right). The mounded elevation of Indian Hill Cemetery and its Russell Chapel are seen at

the west end of Washington Park. The five large buildings of Wesleyan University's Brownstone Row (now known as College Row) fronted the quadrangle lawn that dominated the center of the street. At this time, High Street was fully developed as the premier residential enclave of Middletown and would maintain its renowned character as a street of fine homes well into the 20th century. (AM.)

This 1868 photograph was taken from the cupola of the Nathan Starr Jr. House by Middletown photographer Joseph Bundy. The Joseph Hall House, moved from High Street to College Street to make way for the erection of the Starr House, is seen at lower right. The photograph captures the broadening of the Connecticut River that formed Middletown's harbor and the river's narrowing passage between the hills to the south. (MCHS.)

This view from High Street toward the great bend of the Connecticut River was painted after 1827, the year the Mansion House, the long building in the center, is believed to have been built to include a hotel by Samuel D. Hubbard. In the 1700s, the view would have included ships rounding the bend bearing human cargo from Africa and the Caribbean, a source of wealth for many of the town's inhabitants. (MCHS.)

PROSPECT HOUSE and PALESTINE GARDEN, Middletown Con.

Perhaps Middletown's first planned park, Heth Camp's enclosed Palestine Garden of 1828–1831 was opposite the new Wesleyan University. From his High Street Prospect House overlooking the town, Camp invited citizens to tour (at 12.5¢ each) the gardens for rest and contemplation among exotic plants from the Holy Land. Camp also offered music, balloon ascensions, and a gazebo with a bathhouse. A bath cost 25¢. (MCHS.)

Photographs of the view from High Street were often taken from the roof of Wesleyan's new Judd Hall of Natural Science, constructed in 1871. A reporter wrote that the view was "the finest in the Connecticut Valley, south of Mount Holyoke, and comprises some of the most varied and beautiful scenery in New England." Prospect House is in the foreground. (MCHS.)

In 1861, Mayor Edward Augustus Russell, a High Street resident, renovated Washington Park, formerly known as West Green. The fountain, pictured in 1886, was at the east end of the park that fronted High Street. Fire hydrants and telegraph wiring represent recent improvements. As early as 1850, Charles Alsop, who lived in the house to the left, lobbied for an improved water system with "fountains playing in High Street." (WULSCA.)

Washington Park was the site of promenades, parade musters, fireworks, concerts, and agricultural fairs. In the 1870s, Wesleyan students solemnly marched down High Street to the park, where they would cremate effigies representing unpopular subjects and burn their books. A baseball diamond hosted Wesleyan's first team, the Agallians, Middletown's Forest City Club, and early on, the semiprofessional Mansfields. The T. Macdonough Russell House is at left. (MRL.)

Washington Park has been the preferred location for most of Middletown's war memorials and is now known as Veterans' Memorial Green. In 1904, this monument was erected to honor Connecticut volunteers of the 24th Regiment who saw action in four Civil War battles. The Neoclassical granite design with unusual flanking seats was designed by Middletown native Henry Hilliard Smith, who also designed Colonial Revival–style homes in Middletown. (MRL.)

Washington Park connected High Street with the north entrance to Indian Hill Cemetery, designed by Horatio Stone in 1850. Many High Street families are interred here with elaborate mausoleums and monuments crowning the garden cemetery atop the hill that once was the enclave of Wangunk Native Americans. The Gothic funeral chapel was donated by Frances Russell in 1867 in memory of her husband, Samuel, and her two deceased stepsons. (WULSCA.)

By the time this panoramic view was made in 1909, Wesleyan University's Brownstone Row dominated High Street. Its lawn, manicured with the introduction of powered mowers, planted

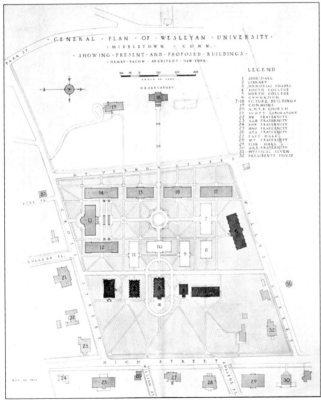

In architect Henry Bacon's 1913 proposal to expand the campus, the partially defined quadrangle of open space was bordered by a portion of Cross Street (later eliminated) to the south and "Wyllys Street" to the north. His master plan would have created a second, more traditional quadrangle to the west of Brownstone Row. The plan was only partially implemented, but it showed how new fraternity buildings along Cross and High Streets would serve to visually enclose the original college quadrangle. (WULSCA.)

with a variety of trees, and crisscrossed by paved "asphaltum" walks that followed student's footpaths, slopes gently to High Street on the left. (LC)

Duane Barnes, who ornamented his Gothic house on High Street with naturalistic plantings, as promoted by the landscape architect Alexander Jackson Downing, led the effort to plant trees on the street and throughout Middletown. Eventually, a double row of majestic elms lined each side of the street in imitation of New Haven's Hillhouse Avenue. Barnes, Simeon North, and other High Street residents promoted tree plantings on the barren drill grounds of the American Literary, Scientific, and Military Academy, inherited by Wesleyan University. North donated trees, as well as his groundsman's labor to plant them, in 1831, and from 1841 to 1862, sophomore students spent "tree day" each year supplementing these. This allée of elms led from Wesleyan's North College dormitory down to High Street. (MCHS.)

High Street
looking south

High Street looking North

In 1870, George B. Goode (Wesleyan class of 1870) made a number of artistic cameo photographs of High Street. A naturalist at heart, he wrote about his rambles throughout the Connecticut Valley in Wesleyan's student newspaper, the *College Argus*. Goode's days on High Street inspired him to pursue a career as a scientist. After working at the US Fish Commission, he returned to campus as curator of the natural history Wesleyan Museum in the new Judd Hall, which was named for Orange Judd. Goode married Judd's daughter, Sarah Ford Judd, in 1877 and left Middletown, later to become a director of the US National Museum, Smithsonian Institution. He was a prominent ichthyologist, planned many international exhibitions for the Smithsonian, and published widely. A genus of split fin fish is named in his honor. (Both, MCHS.)

George B. Goode also recorded for posterity the famous Alsop Elm at the northwest corner of High and Washington Streets in front of Charles Alsop's home. North High Street was constructed through the Alsop property to the right of the grand elm tree soon after this photograph was taken. Goode developed photographic methods to record the natural specimens of fish and other marine life that he collected. (MCHS.)

Middletown, Conn. High Street from Washington St.

Ossian Dodge, a reporter from Cleveland (known as the "Forest City"), visited High Street in 1862, and wrote home that "it almost rivals Euclid Street in Cleveland. It only lacks width." Dodge called Middletown "the Forest City of New England," and the name stuck. A fraternal lodge, baseball team, and many local businesses adopted the nickname. (MRL.)

21

Many photographers came to document High Street's beauty. The Pach brothers of New York opened a satellite studio on Wesleyan's campus, supplying students with a record of their time in Middletown. Above is a c. 1870 Pach view of the university's quadrangle lawn where it met High Street opposite William Street. The street is uneven and unpaved, like most country roads. In the later view below, looking north from Court Street, with the Edward Augustus Russell House on the right, a lone horse-drawn buggy enjoys a better surface. The street has been widened and graded, and granite curbing installed. (Both, MCHS.)

Natural disasters and man-made inflictions led to the denuding of High Street's once majestic, leafy canopy. Ice storms, as pictured above in 1891, and Dutch elm disease (starting in the 1930s) took their tolls. The 1938 New England hurricane was a more sudden shock to the street's natural beauty. Looking toward Delta Kappa Epsilon, the photograph below was taken from the roof of the President's House. Prior to that, trees were lost when the street was widened and macadamized in 1895. Telegraph and power lines that required constant tree pruning, however, were causes of change in the avenue's streetscape over time. Tree replanting programs by Wesleyan and the Middletown Garden Club (2015) have restored some of what has been lost, but smaller trees are now typically selected. (Above, MCHS; below, WULSCA.)

By the early 20th century, with the expansion of Wesleyan, the introduction of automobiles, and improved city services, the scale of High Street buildings grew. Improvements that facilitated this change were welcomed, but the street's character was forever altered. Starting in the 1870s, water and sewer pipes replaced wells and private drains. Electric streetlights replaced occasional gas lampposts, and utility poles strung with wires proliferated. High Street residents resisted an effort to run trolley lines down the boulevard, but progress was hard to mitigate. Automobile traffic lights at Court, College, and Church Street intersections followed. The bucolic view looking south (above) contrasts with the later view below. Old hitching posts and carriage mounting blocks are remnants of the street's residential past, overwhelmed in scale by, from left to right, the new Delta Kappa Epsilon, Fisk Hall, and Psi Upsilon. (Above, MCHS; below, AM.)

The natural ravine, originally part of the Samuel C. Hubbard estate, was later owned by Robert G. Pike, a prominent attorney. His children developed the land to the north in the early 20th century. However, in 1911, local conservationist and philanthropist Col. Clarence Wadsworth bought the ravine and turned it over to the city. The *Middletown Trail Guide* describes the 19 acre preserve at High Street's south end as "a noteworthy oasis of biodiversity." (MCHS.)

Formerly the site of Wesleyan University founder Laban Clark's home (left) until 1867, the school granted access over this land in 2003 for a vest-pocket park (right), connecting High Street with City School Field to the east. Renamed to honor Middletown postmaster Daniel McCarthy, the 2.5 acres between Church and Loveland Streets was the location of memorable athletic contests and has been improved thanks to community efforts. (Left, MRL; right, AM.)

Wesleyan English literature professor Caleb Winchester constructed his High Street house in 1889. In his 1902 textbook *Some Principles of Literary Criticism*, Winchester cited the view from his study of "the whole broad-lying landscape . . . the broad expanse of the river . . . and below and in front the roofs of the city," and the associations this view inspired, as an example of the "emotion of the beautiful" in literature. (MCHS.)

Zadel Barnes grew up in her parent's High Street Gothic house and, years later, reminisced in *Harper's* magazine about her childhood spent in her father's library bay window looking out "to a river glimmering at isolated intervals through intervening foliage." High Street inspired Barnes to read Walter Scott's Waverley novels and to become a writer herself. A nonconformist and social reformer, she was grandmother to the author Djuna Barnes. (AM.)

Two

Houses, Villas, and Mansions

In his 1857 book *Villas & Cottages*, Calvert Vaux, architect of New York's Central Park, touted Middletown as "unquestionably one of the most pleasant and attractive neighborhoods in which to build a country seat to be found in the Eastern States." He attributed Middletown's "refined rural character" to attractive streets carefully adorned with shade and specimen trees.

During Middletown's early history, the dirt road that became High Street developed like other lanes emanating from the town's center, with colonial farmsteads supporting large families. Capt. William Redfield's grandchildren recalled that his place on High Street was surrounded by fruit trees and vegetable gardens that supplied the neighborhood.

By 1825, there were 20 houses and outbuildings on High Street. Only four of these are houses that are known to exist. Three were moved off the street. Most of the other wood-framed structures were demolished in the 19th century to make way for new, more fashionable brick, brownstone, or stuccoed suburban villas built by Middletown's growing elite of foreign traders, merchants, and manufacturers. These men and their wives were encouraged by mid-century builders' pattern books and design guides, which introduced new architectural revival styles. The vernacular Colonial houses, built by master joiners and masons, were replaced by architect-designed, high-style expressions of culture and status, often influenced by stylistic trends seen in New Haven. Popular books by horticulturist Andrew Jackson Downing and others demonstrated how the architecture of these suburban houses could pleasantly complement picturesque landscaping. Rustic farmyards were replaced with exotic garden oases—rarified retreats from their owners' mills and downtown's business bustle.

Starting in the 1860s, the villas were supplemented with mansions reflecting new wealth accumulated by Middletown's barons of industry. After 1900, however, the expanding Wesleyan campus led to an exodus of many old families to Middletown's countryside, where they planned rural estates and gentlemen farms. Meanwhile, houses left behind were sold or given to the university or repurposed by the proliferating fraternities. Others were demolished for new side streets, and once gracefully landscaped estates were subdivided for developments to meet the needs of Middletown's growing middle class.

In this early-19th-century watercolor, Anne Watkinson depicted about 10 houses along High Street at top. The First Congregational Church, formerly at the left end of the ridge, has been replaced by the new church of 1799, seen below on Main Street. Original home lots between High and Main Streets would soon be subdivided and crossed by Broad, Pearl, and Hamlin Streets. (MCHS.)

Built by tailor Edward Rockwell around 1737, this is the earliest known extant High Street house. Its center chimney and double overhangs were typical of early Connecticut architecture. About 1873, the Rockwell House was moved from its original site on the west side of High Street, just north of the Davison Health Center, to Pine Street by builder Henry Fountain, who developed the street along with Fountain Avenue. (JG.)

The old dwelling above, with its center chimney and pronounced roof overhang, was on the west side of High Street south of old Cross Street. The inscribed stone below removed from its fireplace, with a monogram of JSA and a star, confirms the house was built in 1722 by Joseph and Abigail Starr. This land was deeded to his father, Comfort Starr, in 1675. Starr was the town tax collector. He and his son Joseph, like Edward Rockwell, were tailors. The house remained in the family until 1810, but Starr descendants played an important role in the development of High Street. The house was demolished in 1883 to make way for a Wesleyan fraternity, Alpha Delta Phi. Frank Farnsworth Starr, the family's genealogist, photographed the stone. (Both, MCHS.)

William Van Deursen, a noted sea captain in the West Indies trade, lived on High Street. The diary of Mary Russell describes a gay evening of dancing in the ballroom of his home. He was the surveyor of the customs house and was responsible for supervising inspectors, proofing distilled spirits, registering new vessels, and helping to enforce the nation's new trade regulations that prohibited the importation of enslaved persons. (MCHS.)

Captain Van Deursen's house (left) was on the northwest corner of High Street and Wyllis Avenue. A gaslight post marked the entrance to the avenue, opened about 1853. E.W.N. Starr's house is on the right. Around 1875, the Van Deursen house was moved around the corner onto Wyllis Avenue by his heirs Margaret and William Van Deursen, making way for their cottage and the Charles R.G. Vinal House. (MCHS.)

The gambrel-roofed house above, built by Joseph Hall about 1785, is a fine example of the sophisticated Georgian style made affordable by Middletown's West Indies trade. Like the Rockwell and Van Deursen houses, it was moved off High Street. In 1831, Nathan Starr Jr. relocated it around the corner onto Parsonage (now College) Street. It remains on the five acres that extended to Main Street granted to Joseph's grandfather Richard Hall, an original proprietor. In 1849, Starr deeded the house to daughter Mary and her husband, Dr. Hamilton Brewer. Their son Edward, seen at right with his mother and sister Mary Grace, enlisted in the Connecticut Volunteer Infantry at the start of the Civil War. Like many of his fellow soldiers, he fell ill in camp and died in Virginia on April 2, 1863, just weeks shy of his 21st birthday. (Both, MCHS.)

In 1813, Simeon North from nearby Berlin opened a pistol factory in Middletown and, with his wife, Lydia, moved into the house of his father-in-law, Enoch Huntington, at the southwest corner of High Street and today's Wyllis Avenue. North invented the milling machine, which allowed the manufacture of interchangeable parts in the production of thousands of pistols for the US government for use in the War of 1812 and beyond. (MCHS.)

This view of the Huntington-North House, built around 1763, was painted on a dish by neighbor Margaret Van Deursen in 1853, which was about when Wyllis Avenue was constructed. Earlier, when Simeon North sold land across High Street to Nathan Starr Jr., he included in the deed specific measurements and sight lines ensuring that Starr's new house and landscaping would not obstruct North's cherished view of the Connecticut River valley. (MCHS.)

Heth Camp, a merchant from Durham, engaged local master builder Comfort Starr to design and build this boardinghouse in 1828 at the northeast corner of High Street and the newly opened William Street. It had symmetrical side wings and two full-height porticoes in the Roman Doric order. One portico fronted High Street and one faced out over the valley. Camp's Prospect House introduced Palladian-styled urbanity to High Street when it opened to boarders in the spring of 1829. The house looked over Camp's Palestine Garden, where fruits and vegetables were harvested to serve his guests. The grand house was the home to many private academies, and later served different functions for Wesleyan, known as Webb Hall and then East Hall. Although it played a starring role in High Street's history, the site is now Wesleyan's underground power plant. (Both, WULSCA.)

Nathan Starr Jr. built his Federal-style house in 1831 of gray granite from downriver Haddam. After buying this prime site on High Street from Simeon North, Starr moved the Joseph Hall house to Parsonage Street. The replacement, a much admired stone mansion that Starr probably designed, was built by mason Isaac Sage and joiner Israel Russell of Cromwell for $7,800 (equivalent to about a quarter million dollars today). (WULSCA.)

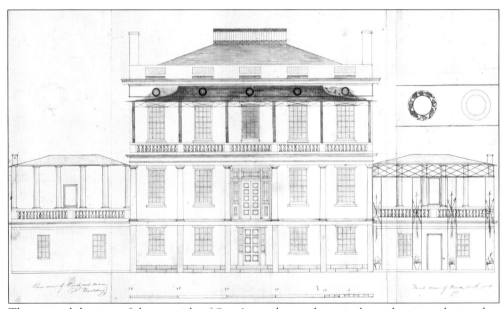

The original drawing of the east side of Starr's new house shows its low side wings, designed so as not to obstruct views from Simeon North's house across High Street. There were two levels of piazzas across the rear from which to enjoy the panorama of the river valley below. The sketches over the drawing were probably done by Nathan's son Elihu, later contemplating some fashionable improvements. (MCHS/JG.)

Itinerant artist Ambrose Andrews painted his masterpiece group portrait of Grace and Nathan Starr Jr.'s children about 1835 in their High Street home, including a view of Middletown and the river beyond. From left to right, the five children, Henry (nine), Frederick (six), Edward (three), Emily (fifteen), and Grace (twelve), are playing battledore and shuttlecock, a game similar to badminton. Little Edward points heavenward, a possible allusion to his recent death. (MMA.)

Nathan and Grace Starr's portraits (hers by Ambrose Andrews in 1835) enjoyed a prominent place in their home. Starr and his father, Nathan Sr., manufactured swords and rifles. Their factory at Staddle Hill innovated the manufacturing technique of the assembly line, later copied by the federal government at the Springfield Armory. Neighbor Simeon North and the Starrs were among the most important American firearms manufacturers of the early 19th century. (Both, MCHS/JG.)

Samuel Russell began his career as a dry goods merchant in Middletown and later established Russell & Company, the largest commission trading firm in Canton, China, dealing in tea, silks, and opium. New York architects Ithiel Town and Alexander Jackson Davis designed Russell's house on the southeast corner of High and Washington Streets. Columns from the failed Eagle Bank in New Haven, topped with Corinthian capitols, were used on Russell's house, completed by 1830. Davis's engraved view of Russell House (below) and another of Russell's brother-in-law Henry Bowers's house in Northampton, Massachusetts—also by Town & Davis—were the only residences illustrated in the 1831 *Hinton's History and Topography of the United States.* The publication of these illustrations had enormous influence on the development of the Greek Revival style in America. (Above, MCHS; below, AM.)

From Canton in 1827, Russell directed his friend Samuel D. Hubbard to oversee the house's construction to suit the taste of his wife, Frances. The double parlors of the Russell House separated by folding pocket doors were innovations of Town & Davis, replicated in many New York townhouses. For $8,500, master builder David Hoadley of New Haven built the Samuel Russell House, designated a national historic landmark in 2001. (NHM.)

Samuel Russell referred to High Street as "Paradise Row," the ideal location for his new house. A partner in Canton, William Low, wrote Russell to enjoy his retirement on the "highest hill in Middletown City." About 1855, a porch was extended to the south, and the rear portico, once open, was enclosed. New stairs down to the extensive gardens were added, employing fashionable Wickersham wire railings from New York. (WULSCA.)

This rare chest, in which Samuel Russell shipped tea from Canton to Western markets, represents the main basis of his company's profits. Russell shipped teas of varying types and grades in these chests that included labels of his Chinese trading partners, especially those of his friend Houqua. Russell's was the most important 19th-century American Far East export company. Warren Delano Jr., Franklin Delano Roosevelt's grandfather, was a Russell & Company partner. (MCHS/JG.)

Upon his return to Middletown from Canton, Samuel Russell (pictured), with Samuel D. Hubbard, founded Russell Manufacturing Company, maker of suspenders, cartridge belts, and woven goods. With his brother Edward Augustus and others, Russell also invested his China profits in a Northampton silk factory and the Air Line Railroad, and was an early investor in Chicago real estate. He died in 1862, one of Connecticut's wealthiest and most philanthropic men. (MCHS.)

Frances Osborne Russell, Samuel Russell's second wife, continued his philanthropy after his death. In 1873, she purchased the former Christ Church at the corner of Broad and Court Streets, converting it into Russell Memorial Library for the city's free public library. Frances's sister Mary, Samuel Russell's first wife, died tragically at the age of 23, leaving two young sons whom Frances raised with her own son, Samuel Wadsworth Russell. (MCHS.)

Five generations of Russells occupied the High Street home until it was sold to Wesleyan University in 1936. Maintaining a property as large as the Russell House required a dedicated and efficient staff. Pictured by the back staircase are, from left to right, the chauffeur and coachman Burton, two women identified as cooks, and the gardener Gustav Overhysser. The grounds, which consisted of over six acres, contained multiple decorative gardens that required constant care. (WULSCA.)

When this painting was made about 1835, three new houses with colonnades facing the river dominated the east side of High Street: Heth Camp's "Prospect House" (1), Nathan Starr Jr.'s house (2), and the Samuel Russell House (3). When Samuel Russell returned from China in 1831, this would have been his first view of his new house on the hill, just north of the old Rev. Noadiah Russell homestead. (MCHS/JG.)

Edward Augustus Russell built his house in 1842 south of his brother Samuel's home. His villa imitated the English Regency style, then fashionable in New York and New Haven. Edward followed Samuel into business, first in Middletown, then in Petersburg, Virginia; Canton; and New York, rising to become president of Royal Insurance Company. As his house replaced the old Rev. Noadiah Russell homestead, Edward died on the same spot of his birth. (WULSCA.)

Returning to Middletown in 1838, Edward Augustus Russell (left) became active in Middletown affairs. He was mayor from 1859 to 1862, a member of the state legislature, and president of the Charles River Railroad. His grandson Richard De Zeng, seen at right with his trademark gray hat, occupied the house until his death in 1932. He made improvements including some new landscaping, planned by the famous Olmsted brothers, between 1897 and 1902. (Both, MCHS.)

The Russells' associate Samuel D. Hubbard built his house south of the Wesleyan campus, set back from High Street. Hubbard, important in Middletown's development, was a US representative and served as Pres. Millard Fillmore's postmaster general. His Italianate house was remodeled by Judge Robert G. Pike, as seen here. Since demolished, its frontage on High Street was developed when "Home Lawn" Avenue was run through the property in the early 20th century. (WULSCA.)

Called "the Italian Villa," the Richard Alsop IV House on the west side of High Street at the head of Court Street was completed by 1840 by Alsop for his twice-widowed mother, Maria Pomeroy Alsop Dana. Middletown's Alsops made their fortunes trading with the West Indies and in maritime insurance, but Richard moved to Philadelphia and earned his wealth in trade with South America and China, and in banking investments. (WULSCA.)

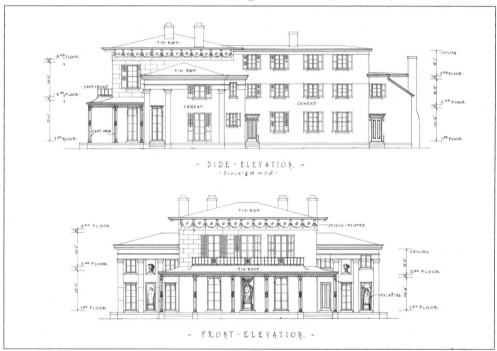

The Richard Alsop IV House is an unusually early example of Greek Revival's transition to the Italianate style. Its architects were Francis Benne (from Germany), Landra Beach Platt, and Sidney Mason Stone of New Haven, with assistance from Philadelphia architect William Strickland. The talk of the town, it was called a "palace" by one visitor. The house was documented by the Historic American Buildings Survey in 1934. (LC.)

The Richard Alsop IV House was designated a national historic landmark in 2009 for the significance of its exterior and interior murals, a rare surviving collection of antebellum decor in Neo-Renaissance style. Alsop sent Philadelphia artist Nicola Monachesi to execute classically inspired paintings with literary themes in tribute to his father, Richard Alsop III, poet and member of the literary Hartford Wits. The painted trompe l'oeil statues in niches (above) were executed when stucco was substituted for marble to save cost. From left to right are the three muses of poetry: Calliope (epic poetry), Erato (love poetry) and Victory (oratory). While Richard Alsop IV died and never lived in the Middletown house, his mother (right); his widow, Aimeé; and his unmarried sister Frances did. Some assumed the three muses represented the three women in Alsop's life. (Above, WULSCA; right, DAC.)

Elihu William Nathan Starr, Nathan Starr Jr.'s son and his partner in Starr Arms, built this house in 1842 on family land at the Court Street corner. E.W.N. Starr (nicknamed "East West North Starr" by children) designed his house in the Tuscan style, emulating the floor plan (with double parlors facing the street) and Italianate details of Richard Alsop IV's house. In the carte de visite below, Starr's sons, from left to right, Henry Barnard, William Edward, and Frank Farnsworth, pose in Civil War uniforms. William enlisted in the Connecticut Volunteer Infantry, was taken severely ill at Harper's Ferry, and honorably discharged. Frank became a noted genealogist, aided by the fact that his father was Middletown's probate judge and town clerk with access to vital records dating to the earliest days of Middletown's settlement. (Left, WULSCA; below, MCHS.)

The northern portion (left) of the brick Italianate home at 118 High Street was likely built by Amos Beckwith before 1851. Beckwith, an abolitionist, was active in the Middletown Anti-Slavery Society. Reform-minded, he withdrew from the Baptist church in 1841, believing it did not support temperance. Eldon Birdsey (Wesleyan class of 1871), a lawyer and Middletown probate judge, later remodeled the house with the library addition to the south. (JG.)

David J. Neale built this unusual three-story Italianate house at 190 High Street, with its distinctive Greek Revival porch, about 1855. Neale and brother Thomas were successful merchant-tailors specializing in ecclesiastical vestments and collegiate robes, with stores in Middletown and New York City. They imported fine cloths and shipped their unique products nationwide. Reportedly, Neale supplied the gowns for the justices of the US Supreme Court. (WULSCA.)

By 1851, Duane Barnes completed construction of this Gothic Revival masterpiece. Built of large Portland brownstone blocks, ornamented with carved wood vergeboard in acorn patterns and ornamental iron details, his house was as startlingly different as the Richard Alsop IV House to its south. Barnes's partner in design and construction was Edwin Rockwell. Both men were Middletown booksellers but also went on to construct Gothic-style houses in Middletown. Barnes's "English Cottage," as it was known, was featured in Andrew Jackson Downing's publication the *Horticulturist*. Barnes sold his house in 1854 to William Sebor, a retired captain of New York–London packet ships. Sebor expanded the house to the south with an addition consistent with the original style. The elevation drawing of the original house is by Stephen J. Roper (Wesleyan class of 1971). (Above, AM; below, courtesy of Stephen J. Roper.)

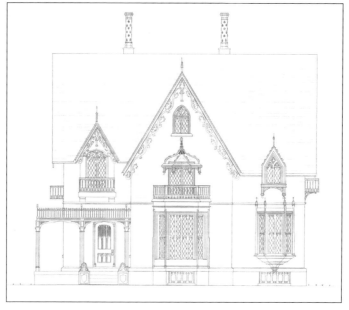

The interior of the Barnes House was as magnificently Gothic as the exterior. Anglophile Duane Barnes, a poet and publisher, had his bookstore on Main Street where Wesleyan students and professors often congregated with townspeople for literary conversation. He lavished special attention on his library (above) at the front of the house, although the curved "bridal" staircase below was also a marvel of craftsmanship. The Sebor family, including many unmarried siblings, occupied the house until 1901. Packet ship master William Sebor was known for having captained Mademoiselle D'Jeck, the famous performing elephant, from England to New York through a violent storm that almost lost the animal overboard. The Art Nouveau wallpaper was probably added by Louis DeKoven Hubbard, whose family lived here until the property was sold to Wesleyan University in 1934. (Both, MCHS.)

Besides his activities as a bookseller and building contractor, Duane Barnes was an abolitionist and civic booster. He promoted railroad lines, the brownstone quarries, and harbor improvements, and planted High Street's double rows of elm trees. He and his wife, Cynthia Turner Barnes, parented 14 free-spirited children with unusual names such as Niar, Unade, and Zadel. Most had remarkable careers in diverse fields, including politics, engineering, writing, and art. (UMD.)

In 1923, Louis DeKoven Hubbard and his family and their pets posed with Louis's new blue Stutz Bearcat behind the Barnes-Sebor House. The Bearcat was considered by some to be America's first sports car. From left to right are son Elijah K. Hubbard III, age 23; two unidentified; Grace Dabney Douglas Hubbard, Louis's wife; and Louis. He died in the house in 1934. (MCHS.)

This Carpenter Gothic house with unusual pendant finials on the southwest corner of High and Washington Streets was likely built by Duane Barnes and Edwin Rockwell about 1852 after a design in Andrew Jackson Downing's 1842 *Cottage Residences*. When T. Macdonough Russell constructed his new house on this site in 1902, George Hennigar moved this house to the corner of High and Lincoln Streets. Hennigar was a successful Middletown photographer. (WULSCA.)

In 1887, George Hulbert expanded and further altered Charles Alsop's house at the northwest corner of High and Washington Streets. Built around 1775, the house originally belonged to Revolutionary War quartermaster Chauncey Whittelsey. By about 1840, Alsop had gothicised the house and added flanking wings, said to be part of Whittelesy's nearby store that Alsop had divided in half and moved. Hulbert, president of Middletown Plate Company, overhauled the house with Swiss-style decorative details and molded brick chimneys. (MCHS.)

After Simeon North's death, his house was purchased by Gabriel Coite, who built this Italianate villa in its place in 1856. The house, similar to others in New Haven designed by architect Sidney Mason Stone, had a curved driveway from High Street, passing through the porte cochere. Coite, a Brooklyn manufacturer of shoe lasts, moved to Hartford to become state treasurer, selling the house to Jane Miles Hubbard (below left), Samuel D. Hubbard's widow. Her niece Susan Clarke (below right) inherited the house. She was a founder of the Wadsworth Chapter, Daughters of the American Revolution; the chapter's first meeting was in the parlor in 1892. Clarke entertained Wesleyan faculty and students here and was a benefactor of the Delta Kappa Epsilon fraternity across High Street. In gratitude, she was made an honorary member. (Above and below right, AM; below left, MCHS.)

Amelia "Minnie" Hotchkiss Vinal and her husband, Charles R.G. Vinal, constructed their Italianate home at the northwest corner of High Street and Wyllis Avenue about 1875. Its distinctive balcony with canopy, box bay windows, and bracketed pediments are very similar to the King-North House in New Haven and may have been designed by the same architect, Henry Austin, who also designed Rich Hall for Wesleyan University. (WULSCA.)

The Vinals pose slightly apart in their side yard, showing the view of the Connecticut River, visible even after Professor Caleb Winchester constructed his house opposite theirs in 1889. Attorney Charles Vinal (Wesleyan class of 1861) served in the Civil War with the 24th Connecticut Regiment and was Middletown's mayor and secretary of the state of Connecticut (1901–1905). Vinal Vocational-Technical High School is named after the Vinals. (Courtesy of Clive Conner.)

This modest Gothic vernacular cottage, with French doors opening onto the front porch, was built by Margaret Van Deursen (below right) about 1873 on the lot inherited from her paternal grandfather, Capt. William Van Deursen. A spinster, she and her unmarried brother William, a Civil War veteran and dog lover (below left), lived here after moving the family's colonial home around the corner onto Wyllis Avenue. The cottage stands today, although much altered, between the houses of Charles R.G. Vinal and Richard Alsop IV. Margaret honored the legacy of her family on High Street by gifting Van Deursen furniture, paintings, and archival material to the Middlesex County Historical Society. However, she struck Wesleyan University from her will when it was discovered that a student stole her favorite cat to be a laboratory specimen. (All, MCHS.)

The gardens of Sarah Gildersleeve Fife were the showpiece of her home (center), formerly that of Margaret Van Deursen. Fife was a founder of the Middletown Garden Club, and after relocating to New York City was the president of the Garden Clubs of America and head of the advisory council of the New York Botanical Garden. An avid bibliophile, Sarah Fife helped found the Hroswitha Club for female book collectors. The rear of the Charles R.G. Vinal House is at right. (MRL.)

This Queen Anne–style home at the northeast corner of High and Washington Streets, with elaborate terra-cotta and brick details, was built about 1892 by D. Luther Briggs, a meat wholesaler and mayor of Middletown from 1890 to 1894. Phillip Stueck, who purchased the home in 1919, worked with his father, Jacob, in the catering business and built Stueck's Modern Tavern on lower Washington Street. (MCHS.)

Samuel C. and Caroline Hubbard built this house and barn in 1866 after acquiring 10 acres of high ground at the south end of High Street overlooking a natural gorge (later known as Pike's Ravine). The design was taken from Calvert Vaux's 1857 pattern book *Villas and Cottages*. Hubbard, who served as mayor soon after moving in, probably dammed the creek to create the picturesque pond. In 1883, the unpopular president of Wesleyan, John Beach, purchased the estate. His move here, a quarter mile from campus, was controversial and did not help his poor relationship with students. In 1887, the newspaper reported that he had forcibly removed a student he found skating on the pond. Soon after, he was "rotten egged" by students; such incidents, among others, led to his removal by Wesleyan's trustees later that year. (Both, MCHS.)

Samuel C. Hubbard's brother-in-law and business partner Gaston Tryon Hubbard constructed an equally grand new mansion next door in 1869. It was reported to have cost a staggering $55,000. Since 1851, the two men had a successful riverfront business, Hubbard Brothers, purveyors of building supplies. Their houses in the then-fashionable Eastlake and Mansard styles would have been good advertisements for their products. Gaston's was quite similar to two designs in New Haven by architect Henry Austin. The stunning Gothic-style conservatory to the rear of Gaston Hubbard's house was probably erected by Orange Judd, who occupied the house in the 1870s. Judd (Wesleyan class of 1847) was a New York publisher of agricultural magazines and books, including many on greenhouse construction. After overseeing construction of Judd Hall of Natural Science at his alma mater nearby, he settled in Middletown. (Both, MCHS.)

The Gaston Tryon Hubbard mansion was later the home of James H. and Mary Hubbard Bunce. At the age of 19, Bunce embarked on a lifelong career in retail. Moving to Middletown in 1856, he worked for other concerns before launching his own establishment. The James H. Bunce Company, with 56,000 feet of floor space, was a mainstay of Main Street until the mid-1970s. Bunce's children sold the estate to Walter French in what a local newspaper described as "one of the most important real estate transactions in Middletown history." After 1924, French razed the house and developed a new street with houses stepping up the hill, called Mansfield Terrace. To the north, Gaston Hubbard's sons Gaston Tracy and Fred Perry Hubbard built a Georgian Revival mansion in 1896 (below). The brothers ran Rogers & Hubbard, manufacturing ivory goods and bone fertilizer. (Left, MCHS; below, MRL.)

Mary and William W. Wilcox Jr. built their Shingle-style house, designed by local architect Jasper D. Sibley, near the southwest corner of High Street and Lawn Avenue by 1890. The Wilcoxes had three acres of gardens along Lawn Avenue. By the time of the home's construction, the family business Wilcox, Crittenden & Company, founded by William W. Wilcox Sr., was the nation's largest and most diversified manufacturer of marine hardware. Wilcox Sr. had ensured the success of the venture by marketing the company's main product, the metal grommet, as far north as Halifax. The firm also made ship portholes, steering wheels, anchors, and lights along with a vast array of other marine products. By 1961, the company was a division of North & Judd, and the forge could still be heard operating by nearby Pameacha Pond. (Above, WULSCA; below, MRL.)

In 1903, Mary Wells French, a widow, constructed this house for herself and her daughter Martha's family. Martha Sherman French married Thomas Hoops Jr., a Chicago mechanical engineer. Hoops relocated to Middletown in 1899 to superintend the Wilcox, Crittenden & Company, where he patented the firm's well-known Ereful boat whistle. It is likely that Henry Hilliard Smith, a Middletown native, designed the Craftsman-style French-Hoops house. (JG.)

Mason William Mylchreest immigrated to Middletown from the Isle of Man in 1869. Mylchreest and his sons William Jr. and Joseph built homes and many Wesleyan buildings on High Street. These two homes (built around 1895) between Church and Loveland Streets are evidence of the family's skill with brickwork. The house on the left served as the parsonage for the nearby German Evangelical Lutheran Church, which Mylchreest also constructed in 1896. (MRL.)

This imposing Neo-Federal house was constructed about 1893 by Elijah Kent Hubbard Jr. between the Alsop and Barnes houses. Hubbard's father, Elijah Kent Hubbard Sr., a Middletown native, was a pioneer developer of Chicago. Hubbard Jr. had a coal, grain, and lumber business there but returned to Middletown in 1885. After 1891, he succeeded his uncle Henry G. Hubbard as president of Russell Manufacturing Company. The house was destroyed by fire in 1915. The young boys pictured below about 1905 on the front steps were the scions of Middletown's prominent families. Julius Wadsworth (third row, right), the son of Col. Clarence Wadsworth, grew up to be a foreign service officer. Thomas Macdonough Russell Jr. (front), became an executive at Russell Manufacturing Company and a prominent civic leader. (Above, WULSCA; below, MCHS.)

In 1902, T. Macdonough Russell built this brick Southern Colonial mansion across High Street from his great-grandfather Samuel Russell's Greek Revival home. He was Middletown's mayor from 1908 to 1910. The intersection of High and Washington Streets could rightly be called "Mayor's Corner." Samuel Russell Sr. occupied the old house while mayor (1896–1898), and diagonally opposite lived mayors D. Luther Briggs (1890–1894) and Charles Alsop (1843–1846). (WULSCA.)

T. Macdonough Russell (left) was named after his great-grandfather Commodore Thomas Macdonough, the hero of the 1814 Battle of Lake Champlain. A sailor himself, he was commodore of the Middletown Yacht Club. His brother Samuel Russell Jr., pictured in costume in 1897, acquired 400 acres in Middletown's Westfield section. He raised baby beef, sheep, and purebred cows on his Ridgewood Farm. (Left, courtesy of Samuel Russell; right, MCHS.)

In the Gothic room of the 1855 north wing of the Samuel Russell House, lucky visitors could view the collection of maritime memorabilia assembled by T. Macdonough Russell Sr. In addition to many ships' models, including one of the USS *Saratoga*, flagship of Commodore Thomas Macdonough, the collection included shipping documents detailing Samuel Russell's China trade and Middletown's role in the West Indies trade, along with records of over 2,400 ships. (WULSCA.)

The Russell cottage, a Cape Cod–style home, was built between the Samuel Russell and Edward Augustus Russell houses by Thomas Macdonough Russell Jr. and his wife, Marjorie. Family lore tells the story of four-year-old Thomas III crawling out of a second-story window and walking to St. Sebastian Church on Washington Street in search of the family maid Iris. The home was sold to Wesleyan in 1934. (WULSCA.)

This late Italianate home at the corner of High and Church Streets was originally built about 1865 in the Second Empire (or Mansard) style by Seth H. Butler, president of the First National Bank. When Salvatore and Angelina Saraceno purchased it in 1946, they removed its tower, changed the roof lines, and added stucco, reminiscent of architecture in their native Sicily. Saraceno was the treasurer of the popular movie theater on Main Street, the Capitol, as well as a beer wholesaler. They were an elegant couple, pictured at left on their wedding day, November 25, 1914. The Saraceno home contained three apartments, one of which was occupied by Marian Drury, the aunt of Allen Drury, author of *Advise and Consent*, for which he won the Pulitzer Prize for Fiction in 1960. (Both, courtesy of Josephine Saraceno Vassallo.)

Three

HIGH STREET ACADEMIES

Children in colonial America were taught to read so they could be well-versed in the scriptures. It was no different in early Middletown. Proprietor records indicate that the town voted to hire a schoolmaster in 1675, only 25 years after the founding of the town. The following year, the classes were held in the watch-house, a lookout structure. Rev. Enoch Huntington of First Church conducted religious studies at his High Street house.

Over the years, both a town school district and a city school district developed, with 18 schools in the town district and four in the city district, many of them one-room buildings. The first classes of Middletown High School, the oldest public high school in Connecticut, were held in 1840 in the basement of Christ Church, now Russell Memorial Library, two blocks east of High Street.

A number of private academies opened to supplement the public schools, many of them located on beautiful High Street. The bucolic setting and the widening reputation of Wesleyan University attracted students from across Connecticut and beyond. Wesleyan students often served as private tutors. Daniel H. Chase, Wesleyan's first graduate, opened his own school, the Middletown Institute, on Main Street in 1835.

Large houses on High Street served well as private school sites. Heth Camp's estate opposite Wesleyan's grounds was well adapted for four different academies. The Nathan Starr house was home to Reverend Colton's boys' academy, and later, a school for young ladies. In 1884, the Wilson Grammar School was opened by Edwin H. Wilson in the old Charles Alsop (Whittelsey-Hulbert) House at the corner of Washington Street. By 1886, Wilson's Grammar School occupied the Gaston Hubbard house. Elizabeth and Anna Patten operated their school in the E.W.N. Starr house until 1911.

While High Street was associated with many private academies during the 19th century, few lasted long. Capt. Alden Partridge's American Literary, Scientific, and Military Academy suffered the same fate but left a lasting physical imprint on High Street. Its original buildings were adopted by the new Wesleyan University in 1831, the educational institution that would shape the avenue forever.

In this detail of the painting on page 11, the First Congregational Church is visible at top left on the ridge. In 1715, the church was constructed on High Street west of the current intersection with Church Street. In the nearby parsonage, Rev. Enoch Huntington conducted religious studies, perhaps High Street's earliest "school." Huntington tutored Timothy Dwight, who later served as president of Yale (after Huntington declined the position). Enoch was the brother of Samuel Huntington, Connecticut governor, president of the Continental Congress, and signer of the Declaration of Independence. Enoch Huntington and his wife, Mary (below), owned enslaved people, one being a black woman named Jenny. Their house gave Parsonage Street its name (renamed College Street in 1857). It was later occupied by Simeon North, the gunmaker who married the reverend's daughter Lydia. (Above, CHS; below, MCHS.)

The original Russell homestead on High Street was painted around 1835 with the Samuel Russell House to the left. Five Russell generations lived here, including Noadiah Russell, second pastor of the High Street church, teacher, and a founder of Yale College. His son William Russell was the first alumnus of Yale to be elected its rector and served as third pastor of the church. (MCHS.)

The spacious Greek Revival double parlors of Heth Camp's Prospect House served academies well throughout the 19th century. The first was Maple Grove, a "family school" opened in 1831 by Isaac Webb, a Yale graduate and one of Wesleyan's first trustees. Twenty boys between ages 8 and 12 were taught subjects, preparing them for college or business. The yearly cost was $250, covering tuition, language instruction, board, fuel, lights, and washing. (WULSCA.)

CATALOGUE
OF THE
PUPILS
OF
ISAAC WEBB
AND
JULIUS S. SHAILER'S
FAMILY SCHOOL,

MAPLE GROVE,
MIDDLETOWN, CONN.

WILLIAM D. STARR, PRINTER
1841

Isaac Webb's catalogue of students featured a woodcut illustration of the Maple Grove school and garden with early Wesleyan University buildings in the background. Students attended from across the country, including China trader Robert Olyphant; Eli Whitney Jr.; the painter James A. Suydam; James Bulloch, the Confederate States' foreign agent and Theodore Roosevelt's uncle; Charles H. Crane, the surgeon general who attended to Abraham Lincoln upon his assassination (and whose father, Ichabod, was the namesake for the character in Washington Irving's novel *The Legend of Sleepy Hollow*). Webb's most famous pupil was future president Rutherford B. Hayes, who attended the school in 1837 and 1838. His marks in Greek and Latin grammar are entered in the grade book below. (Both, MCHS.)

Isaac Webb and his wife, Mary, kept strict student attendance at church services and meals, recording every infraction. While they stated that "a Family School should not be made a 'Botany Bay,'" their prospectus sternly warned that "no one of vicious habits, and exerting hurtful influence upon his companions, will be allowed to remain in the family." Transgressions were meticulously noted in their Black Book. Henry Huntington from Norwich, Connecticut, was a particular disciplinary nightmare for the Webbs. His aggressions quickly led to expulsion in September 1834. After his only child and wife died, Isaac Webb brought in Julius Shailer and his wife, Catherine Read Shailer, to assist him. The school closed in 1841 after Isaac Webb, ill after travel to the Middle East, committed suicide in 1842 by jumping into Long Island Sound from the stern of the steamboat *Kosciusko*. (Both, MCHS.)

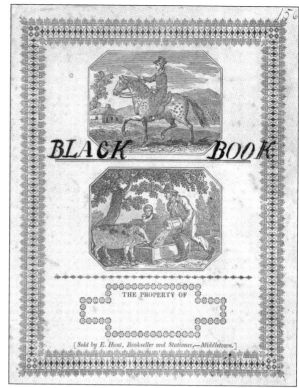

In 1857, Rev. Henry Martyn Colton opened a Classical and English School for boys of any age in the Nathan Starr Jr. House. Colton advertised instruction in Latin, Greek, French, German, and Spanish with "special attention paid to music, drawing, penmanship and other accomplishments." Students could also attend Wesleyan lectures. After Colton's death, his wife, Lucy Tuttle Colton, operated the academy as Mrs. Colton's School for Young Ladies and Children until 1875. (AM.)

Henry Martyn and Lucy Tuttle Colton were well connected with New England's intelligentsia. The Coltons corresponded with Oliver Wendell Holmes and other literary figures. Historian and philosopher John Fiske, a Middletown native, was a frequent visitor. Henry Colton, a Yale graduate, steered his students to the New Haven college, and the couple also opened the Yale School for Boys in New York City. (Courtesy of family of John Colton Wells III.)

The Nathan Starr Jr. House was later the setting for a novel, serving as the home of the Lennox family in *Half Married* (1887) by Annie Bliss McConnell. In *The Children of the Old Stone House* (1911), author Lucy Colton Wells, the Coltons' daughter, also used the Starr House as the romantic setting for her fictional stories of the children's lives at the school on Davenport's "Elm Street." (MCHS.)

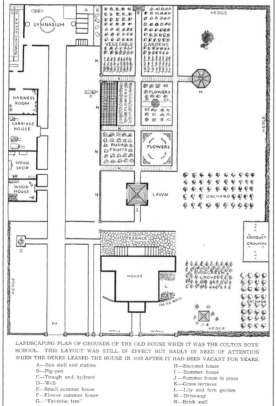

LANDSCAPING PLAN OF GROUNDS OF THE OLD HOUSE WHEN IT WAS THE COLTON BOYS' SCHOOL. THIS LAYOUT WAS STILL IN EFFECT BUT BADLY IN NEED OF ATTENTION WHEN THE DEKES LEASED THE HOUSE IN 1883 AFTER IT HAD BEEN VACANT FOR YEARS.

A—Box stall and stables
B—Pig-pen
C—Trough and hydrant
D—Well
E—Small summer house
F—Flower summer house
G—"Favorite tree"
H—Enclosed house
I—Summer house
J—Summer house in pines
K—Grass terraces
L—Lily and fern garden
M—Driveway
N—Brick wall

Lucy Colton Welles, who fondly remembered her parents' school, included in her book this map of the Starr House grounds, which were extensively landscaped with vegetable and flower gardens, an orchard, and ornamental outbuildings. The school boasted a greenhouse, gymnasium, and even a bowling alley. While Welles's mother, Lucy, taught many daughters of High Street families, the school was eventually difficult to sustain with the rise of free public education. (AM.)

In 1875, James Bradford, superintendent of the Connecticut Industrial School for Girls in Middletown, opened a military school for boys in the Heth Camp House. Called Bradford's Students' Home, the *College Argus* noted sarcastically that the "inmates . . . are sadly afflicted with an irruption of brass buttons." Rev. Barrett Smith next operated it as a "select school for younger children," according to the 1884 *History of Middlesex County*, followed by Elizabeth and Anna Patten's school, which occupied the house from 1883 to 1889. (WULSCA.)

After a brief use of part of the Whittelsey-Hulbert House, Edwin Wilson, also a principal of the public Central School, opened Mr. Wilson's Grammar School in the Gaston Hubbard Mansion. He catered to boarders and day scholars, and by 1887, the school had 36 students. Many High Street parents elected either a general or college course for their sons, later described by a journalist as "lads who are leaders now." (MCHS.)

Georgianna Minor opened a kindergarten in her family's home, the 18th-century Moore House, purchased in 1866 by her father, John Minor. The house remained in the Minor family until sold to Wesleyan in 1974. In 1907, Georgianna Minor posed with her students, including children of the Hubbard, Schaefer, and Nicholson families. At right is blonde Edward "Teddy" Acheson, the son of the rector of Middletown's Church of the Holy Trinity (and future Episcopal bishop of Connecticut), Edward Campion Acheson. Teddy's older brother was Dean Acheson, future secretary of state for Pres. Harry Truman. The youngsters delighted in riding the Hubbards' pony cart up and down High Street (below). From left to right are Otis Hubbard, Lois Smith, Paul Schaefer, Alice Schaefer, two unidentified, and Teddy Acheson. A woman watches from a window at the William W. Wilcox Jr. House. (Both, MCHS.)

In 1824, Middletown lost its bid to host the Episcopalians' new Washington College (now Trinity College in Hartford). However, local leaders were successful in convincing Capt. Alden Partridge to relocate his military academy from Vermont to Middletown. Trustees produced a 13-acre site on High Street. John Lewis, assisted by Merritt Ward and Edward Hine, designed and built the first buildings of Chatham brownstone, the Lyceum and the Barracks. (WULSCA.)

Due to Middletown's more accessible location from Mid-Atlantic and Southern states, Captain Partridge projected growth for his new American Literary, Scientific, and Military Academy. Each year between 1825 and 1829, about 250 cadets came to High Street. However, after being denied accreditation and the ability to raise funds by lottery, Partridge returned the academy to Vermont (now Norwich University). Only the second building from the left was not constructed. (WULSCA.)

In August 1824, Middletown's civic leaders authorized a committee to purchase land and quarry brownstone to erect the first two buildings for Captain Partridge's academy. The original Lyceum building, seen here in 1879, housed an arsenal, laboratory, classrooms, and hall used as a chapel, meeting, and drill room. Later remodeled by Wesleyan for other purposes and known as South College, it is the university's oldest building. (WULSCA.)

The local committee that supervised construction of buildings for the academy included leading citizens of Middletown: Thomas Mather, John Hinsdale, George W Stanley, Elijah Hubbard, John L. Lewis, John Alsop, and Samuel D. Hubbard. The Barracks was one of Middletown's largest buildings. A boarding hall building was also constructed to house a kitchen, dining hall, and officer quarters. This building burned in 1906 and was replaced by North College. (WULSCA.)

This plain brick building was built by Captain Partridge in 1826 for use as a gun storage house for the American Literary, Scientific, and Military Academy. When Wesleyan took over the academy buildings in 1831, the gun house was converted for use as a chemical laboratory. Other later uses were as a chapel, icehouse, carpentry shop, infirmary, and electrical laboratory. Prior to being razed in 1907, it served as the Connecticut Bacteriological Laboratory. (MRL.)

Alden Partridge, once West Point's superintendent, held advanced ideas for combining physical education, scientific military instruction, and liberal arts to prepare young Americans for leadership and engineering of national improvements. Partridge took his Middletown cadets on hikes as far away as Niagara Falls. Cadets also mapped Middletown environs, producing an impressive topographical map of 400 square miles. Graduates included future governors, congressmen, a Navy secretary, engineers, and distinguished lawyers. (WULSCA.)

Edwin Ferry Johnson, a graduate of Partridge's academy, taught mathematics and civil engineering there. An important early proponent of railroads, Johnson engineered many new rail lines, notably the Air Line from Middletown to Boston; lobbied for transcontinental railroads; and engineered the Northern Pacific Railroad. He lived in Middletown for 40 years, serving as mayor. This c. 1825 portrait of Johnson depicts the distinctive cadet's uniform designed by Captain Partridge. (SMNU.)

A natural sciences professor at the academy, Dr. Joseph Barratt remained in Middletown after the school returned to Vermont. An eccentric, obsessive polymath, he lectured on botany at Wesleyan and developed an important herbarium. Barratt believed that some dinosaur footprint fossils found in central Connecticut were those of a four-toed human that he called "Homo Tetradactylos." A slab with fossils marks his grave in Indian Hill Cemetery. (MCHS/JG.)

William Huntington Russell was born in Middletown in 1809, a cousin of Samuel Russell. He attended Captain Partridge's academy between 1826 and 1828, graduated from Yale in 1833, served in the state legislature, and was a major general during the Civil War. Along with Alphonso Taft, he was a founder of the Yale secret society Skull & Bones. Russell is also considered to be one of the founders of the Republican Party. (MCHS.)

In 1844, Henry Colton Shumway painted E.W.N. Starr, another academy graduate, in the uniform of a colonel of the 6th Regiment, Connecticut Militia. Starr organized the Mansfield Guards in 1847, and was elected brigadier general of the 2nd Brigade, Connecticut Militia in 1860. He later commanded the military post in Middletown during the organization of the 24th Connecticut Volunteer Infantry for service in the Civil War. (MCHS/JG.)

Four

THE COLLEGE ON THE HILL

While impressive new homes graced High Street between 1830 and 1875, The Wesleyan University, as it was known until 1870, struggled to survive. Its campus was unkempt and maintenance was deferred on its few buildings. One student wrote home, "The houses here are aristocratic [but] the college looks more like a prison than an institution of learning." At its inception, many local families of different denominations had guided and financially underwritten the new Methodist-affiliated school. A deal to lease Wesleyan the city's interest in its brownstone quarry in Portland, as well as loans from Middletown banks secured by the High Street property, kept the fragile institution afloat.

By 1870, however, fewer local residents served as trustees, ceding influence to presidents, faculty, and church leaders. With support from wealthy Boston and New York alumni donors and a widening reputation in scholastics and athletics, great changes were reflected in the physical plant. The stately Brownstone Row that has become the school's trademark image (now referred to as College Row) was established with the construction of Memorial Chapel and Rich and Judd Halls to the south of the original South and North College buildings. Vincent Scully, architectural historian, wrote that High Street's Brownstone Row is like a fortification, "a splendid urban line drawn along the military crest of the hill so that the first rank of buildings can deploy upon it, facing east across the valley. They take up a commanding position, in fine response to the place."

By 1920, a third of Wesleyan's faculty lived on High Street; a few built their own homes here. In the early 20th century, the campus expanded west and south, away from the street. Nonetheless, High Street was transformed by the construction of fraternities with their popular eating clubs. Some replaced older homes so that, as the college newspaper reported in 1883, "One by one the old landmarks disappear. . . . How strange Middletown would look to an old graduate." By 1950, Wesleyan, which owned almost all property between Washington and Church Streets, acquired many of the remaining landmarks. The old villas would have a new life yet.

The departure of Captain Partridge's academy was a setback for Middletown. However, through the efforts of local reverends Heman Bangs, Laban Clark, and others who served as trustees for the property and pledged funds, the Methodist Church (after considering proposals from Troy and Bridgeport), determined to open The Wesleyan University on the academy's 14-acre High Street site in 1831. The Lyceum and Barracks would see new life as South College and North College. Local builders Barzallai Sage and Isaac Baldwin constructed a house (above right and below) in 1838 for the university's first president, Rev. Willbur Fisk. The simple structure, with double parlors facing High Street, was paid for with a loan from Fisk and proceeds from his 1838 book *Travels in Europe*. Eight Wesleyan presidents occupied the house until 1905 and one, Pres. Stephen Olin, was born here. (Both, WULSCA.)

In 1870, the students of Phi Nu Theta literary society (also known as Eclectic) pose on the west side slope along High Street with South and North Colleges as backdrop. South College contained Wesleyan's chapel, library, and classrooms, but early on, it housed James Russell's Stupendous and Magnificent Planetarium, or Columbian Orrery, a unique mechanical model of the solar system purchased by Wesleyan, which attracted townspeople to the new campus. (WULSCA.)

On March 1, 1906, fire destroyed North College, displacing hundreds of students. Shocked townspeople came the next day to view the charred remains. A new brownstone building was constructed in its place the next year. It featured a pronounced portico that served as a backdrop for graduations until Denison Terrace was constructed to the rear of Olin Library in 1931. North College today houses most of Wesleyan's administrative offices. (WULSCA.)

Memorial Chapel – Wes Univ.

The centerpiece of Brownstone Row, Memorial Chapel, was designed by Nichols & Brown, architects of Albany, New York, and was built between 1868 and 1871. (The architects completed construction of South Congregational Church in 1868, and their First Congregational Church on Court Street was begun in 1871.) Photograph cards of Charles Nichols's rendering for Wesleyan's new chapel were distributed to publicize the $70,000 required to finish the brownstone-clad Gothic Revival church. Most of the funds were raised by Civil War veteran alumni and university-affiliated women celebrating the centenary of Methodism in America. Probably the earliest building constructed to specifically honor those lost in the recent Civil War, the chapel (pictured below in 1893) housed recitation rooms and a second-floor sanctuary, Memorial Hall. Prior to its construction, chapel services were conducted in South College's basement. (Left, MCHS; below, WULSCA.)

Memorial Chapel, Wesleyan University, Middletown, Conn.

Two hundred ninety-eight Wesleyan men served in the Civil War; twenty-four of them with the Confederacy. Thirty-one died in battle or from disease. Stained-glass windows memorializing these men, as well as those who died in World Wars I and II, were added later. The chapel's interior was significantly remodeled in 1916 by architect Henry Bacon when the second floor (above) was replaced with side balconies (below). Beloved professors Caleb Winchester (first row, second from right) and William North Rice (far right) are seen at the last service in the old sanctuary in 1916. Although Wesleyan had ended its Methodist affiliation in 1937, morning chapel attendance was compulsory until 1960. Since then, Memorial Chapel, the heart of the campus, has been the venue for funeral services, weddings, concerts, and important guest lectures. (Both, WULSCA.)

Rich Hall, south of Memorial Chapel (pictured above in 1879), was dedicated as the new university library in 1868 and named for Boston fish merchant and benefactor Isaac Rich. Like the chapel then starting construction, the brownstone building was designed in the Gothic Revival style. Along with the Duane Barnes House and the Russell Library, it is the most important nonecclesiastical structure of this style in Middletown. New Haven architects Henry Austin and David Russell Brown modeled it after Austin's fireproof Dwight Hall Library at Yale. Like Dwight Hall, Rich Hall had book alcoves, but these were individually daylit by windows as requested by President Cummings. Cummings was obsessed with the building's design, from its ventilation chimneys to its adjustable shelves, but lost the battle of styles. His one admonition was "it should not be Gothic." (Both, WULSCA.)

In 1930, two years after Olin Library was constructed with its open stack system, which could accommodate 800,000 books (compared to Rich Hall's 18,000), book alcoves were removed from Rich Hall, and the interior was gutted for a theater (above) through generous donations from the class of 1892. The repurposing for the '92 Theater left only the original wood roof trusses in place. Besides play productions, the space was the site of promenade dances, such as the one pictured below in 1946. In 2003, another renovation converted the traditional theater to a more flexible black box performance venue, funded by the Patricelli family. It is the home of Wesleyan's theater company Second Stage, the second-oldest student-run theater in the United States. In 1999, Second Stage premiered an early version of *In the Heights*, written by Pulitzer Prize– and Tony Award–winner Lin-Manuel Miranda (Wesleyan class of 2002). (Both, WULSCA.)

Judd Hall of Natural Science (left, above) was named for Orange Judd (Wesleyan class of 1847), trustee, proponent of admitting female students, generous donor, and publisher of the widely read *American Agriculturalist*. This Brownstone Row structure, completed in 1871, was one of the first college buildings in America devoted entirely to scientific research and the study of the natural sciences. The chemistry, natural history, and physics departments occupied the lower two floors, while the Wesleyan Museum displayed its vast collection on the upper two floors. Over 100,000 artifacts were collected or donated by students, alumni, and townspeople, including a dinosaur skeleton and Egyptian mummy, under the supervision of the first curator, George B. Goode. Middletown children took field trips to the High Street museum throughout the 1930s. (Both, WULSCA.)

Judd Hall was designed by Boston architects Bryant & Rogers from their Hartford office, overseen by Francis Kimball, considered the father of skyscraper technology. He later designed Middletown's Middlesex Opera House (1892). Five-story Judd Hall was of fireproof construction, using mostly brownstone, slate, and iron. Its chimneys, advanced in design, ventilated laboratory classrooms (below). Through Orange Judd's efforts, the country's first agricultural station was housed here (1875–1877). In 1892, Professor Wilbur Olin Atwater built his famous respiration calorimeter in the basement. It consisted of a chamber in which human subjects lived for up to five days for measurements of metabolism and caloric values of foods and even (controversially) alcohol. Until his death in 1907, almost 500 experiments were conducted here. Judd Hall was completely gutted, and the top floor reconstructed in 1957. (Both, WULSCA.)

ORANGE JUDD HALL OF NATURAL SCIENCE.
Wesleyan University, Middletown, Ct.

85

Originally fronting on Cross Street, Scott Laboratory appears more a part of Brownstone Row since the street was removed in 1928. Designed in the Beaux Arts Classical style by architect Charles Alonzo Rich and originally housing the physics department, it was dedicated in 1904 to the memory of John Bell Scott (Wesleyan class of 1881), who succumbed to fever while serving as a Navy chaplain in the Spanish–American War. (WULCSA.)

The Middletown Scientific Association (1871–1968) was an organization of Wesleyan faculty and residents seeking to promote interest in scientific study among the people in Middletown. The group sponsored excursions to sites of scientific interest and met monthly in Judd Hall or Scott Laboratory to hear papers delivered by members and guest speakers, such as Nobel Prize–winner physicist Enrico Fermi, who spoke on January 11, 1940. (WULSCA.)

Fisk Hall, named after Wesleyan's first president, Willbur Fisk, was built in 1903 by William Mylchreest, who constructed many campus and residential buildings in the High Street neighborhood. It was designed by the New York architectural firm of Cady, Berg, and See in the Renaissance Revival style and was made entirely of Portland brownstone. At one point housing the campus post office and store, it is now the home of the foreign languages department, international studies office, and numerous lecture halls. It was the scene on February 21, 1969, of the Fisk Hall takeover when leaders of the Afro-American Society, students, and Middletown residents barricaded themselves in the building to bring awareness to inequality at the university. Thirteen black students matriculated in 1965 and became known as the Vanguard Class, paving the way for a more diverse student body. (Above, AM; below, WULSCA.)

In 1934, at the cornerstone ceremony for the new Squash Racquets Building north of North College, Ellen Himrod Denison, widow of Charles Denison, a major Wesleyan benefactor, wields the trowel. Looking on are Wesleyan president and future Connecticut governor James McConaughy (left) and donor George Davison (Wesleyan class of 1892). Designed by architects McKim, Mead & White, the only brick building on Brownstone Row was gutted in 2012 and rededicated as Boger Hall for faculty and administrative offices. (WULSCA.)

The starkly contemporary Zelnick Pavilion by Robert Olsen + Associates was constructed in 2003 and connects the Patricelli '92 Theater and Memorial Chapel, altering the silhouette of College Row. (South and North Colleges were previously connected with a more modest glazed entrance.) The pavilion of concrete, steel, and glass serves as a reception space for the theater but also facilitates accessibility to the different levels of the old brownstone buildings. (AM.)

The modern office building above was built in 1961 on the site of the demolished Samuel C. Hubbard home. It housed operations of *My Weekly Reader*, the elementary school magazine acquired by Wesleyan University Press in 1952. Xerox Corporation purchased the magazine in 1965 in exchange for 400,000 shares of its stock. As a result, for a time, Wesleyan was the best endowed college in the country for its size. Funding from that transaction fueled campus growth, including the Center for the Arts (1973), a village of 11 starkly cubic limestone buildings designed by Roche and Dinkeloo Partners (below). Stretching from Wyllys Avenue to Washington Park, the complex backdrops High Street's residential scale. The design plays off the street's immutable classical architecture, especially that of the Richard Alsop IV and Edward Augustus Russell Houses. (Above, JG; below, photograph by William Van Saun.)

By 1908, when this engraving was made of artist Richard Rummell's bird's-eye view of Wesleyan's campus on High Street, the university's domination of the hill was complete. The lone horse and carriage suggests the automobile had not yet made its mark on the avenue. Visible below High Street are the back sides of, from left to right, Eclectic, Webb Hall (Camp House), Psi Upsilon, Fisk Hall, and Delta Kappa Epsilon. Opposite Fisk Hall is the First President's House, and to its right is the second President's House (Coite-Hubbard House). At left facing the quadrangle are

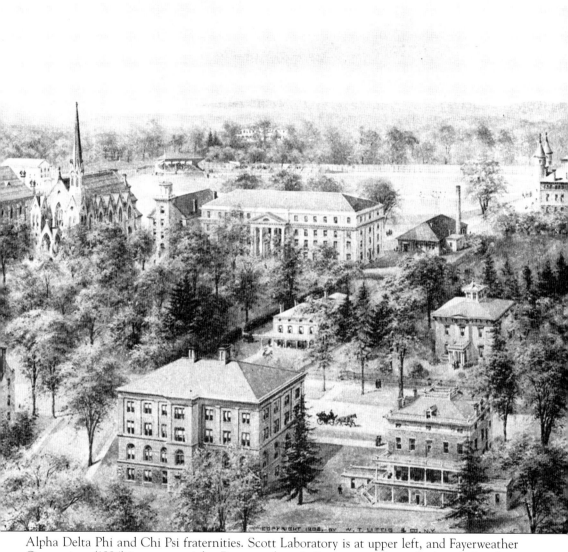

Alpha Delta Phi and Chi Psi fraternities. Scott Laboratory is at upper left, and Fayerweather Gymnasium (1894) is at upper right. Between these is Brownstone Row, which includes, from left to right, Judd Hall, Rich Hall, Memorial Chapel, South College, and North College. In 1839, Wesleyan's first president, Willbur Fisk wrote, "In fact, a flourishing College will of itself, build up a town. If any one doubt this, let him look at Middletown and mark its progress." (WULSCA.)

Whether living in the North College dormitory, such as Room No. 62 pictured above, or in a fraternity clubhouse, student life at Wesleyan was generally like that at most other colleges. However, in the 19th century, some unique High Street traditions developed. An unsightly billboard at the corner of William Street was torched repeatedly. In winter, students enjoyed snow-sledding down the streets all the way to Main Street. Come spring, graduates clad in monk's attire could be seen marching to Washington Park to cremate effigies of "Mathematics." Fraternities, which, by 1890, housed most students, were the scenes of much light-hearted, and sometimes controversial, activity (below). In 1893, Delta Kappa Epsilon brothers Melrose Davies (left) and Frederick Parker (right) induced straight-laced William Anderson (who did not smoke or drink) to pose with them, much to "Andy's" later embarrassment. (Above, WULSCA; below, AM.)

An enduring High Street mystery involves the location at any given time of the 140-pound brass Douglas cannon. Freshman classes fired the cannon to mark the Fourth of July and, later, Washington's Birthday. Sophomores were intent on foiling their efforts, resulting in the legendary "cannon scraps" reported by the national press. The first cannons were left behind by Partridge's academy, but the later cannon was donated by the local W&B Douglas Company. Members of the class of 1889 fired the cannon (above) and three returned 25 years later to do it again before a photographer and boys. "Doug" was stolen and sunk in the Connecticut River in 1880, spiked to a brownstone block between South College and Memorial Chapel in 1931, and disappeared again in 1957. It has since traveled the world. (Both, WULSCA.)

The local Gamma Phi chapter of Delta Kappa Epsilon fraternity purchased the Nathan Starr Jr. House (aka the "Colton House") in 1888. The brothers made significant Neo-Federal-style alterations in 1897, including the addition of a fourth floor and a porch across the front (right). The original rendering by Hartford architects Barrett & Comstock (left) included a more elaborate widow's walk and an elaborate cupola, never executed. (AM/MCHS.)

Even remodeled, it was said that ghosts haunted the old Starr-Colton House. (There are similar recent claims regarding the Samuel Russell House.) In 1929, Delta Kappa Epsilon gutted its old house and added side wings to provide for modern bedrooms and conveniences. New York society architect Aymar Embury II's country house design reflected a more traditional Colonial Revival style in keeping with period tastes. (Courtesy of Katrina Winfield-Howard.)

Delta Tau Delta fraternity, like others, moved from one rented house to another, including the Richard Alsop IV House, pictured here in 1912. Brothers often shared rooms in old High Street homes. Delta Tau Delta next leased the Elijah K. Hubbard House until it was destroyed by fire in 1964, soon after which they constructed the most contemporary of Wesleyan fraternity buildings, 156 High Street, designed by local architect John Martin. (WULSCA.)

Old High Street mansions, even rented, gave fraternity chapters the appearance of legitimacy. Given the competition for freshman recruits, the homey atmosphere of the houses was considered an advantage by many. The Kappa Alpha brothers proudly flew their flag while posing in 1946 at the side yard of the William W. Wilcox Jr. House, which the fraternity owned until 1966, when Wesleyan tore it down for a parking lot. (WULSCA.)

By the 1890s, most Wesleyan students were enrolled in one of the Greek letter clubs, which were the social centers of campus life. This held true through the 1940s and 1950s when Kappa Nu Kappa brothers and their dates in bobby sox occupied the Edward Augustus Russell House, as seen in 1955. The third-floor addition was later removed by Wesleyan, restoring the house closer to its original appearance. (WULSCA.)

The first fraternity to build on High Street was Alpha Delta Phi in 1883, replacing the Joseph Starr house at the corner of Cross Street. Known as the "Ranch," it was designed by fraternity brother Charles Sherman Edgerton (Wesleyan class of 1870). The Van Benschoten house is visible to the left. In 1904, Alpha Delta Phi replaced the house with a grand Georgian Revival brick structure, designed by Charles Alonzo Rich. (MCHS.)

The first intercollegiate fraternity at Wesleyan, Xi Chapter of Psi Upsilon (1843), built its new clubhouse at the southeast corner of High and College Streets in 1891–1893 (above). Designed by English architect Colin Wilson in the Jacobethan Revival style, it was notable for its combination of yellow brick, carved and rusticated brownstone trim, and Cobalt granite base. The house featured special meeting rooms and a lookout over the valley from the stair tower. Many men who lived on High Street, such as Professors Van Benschoten and Winchester and Wesleyan benefactor Orange Judd, were Psi U brothers. In 1927, Chi Psi built its new lodge on Cross Street, seen below, in a style similar to that of Psi Upsilon. As there was a chance that Cross Street would be eliminated, the building was designed with this entrance on Church Street as well. (Above, MCHS; below, WULSCA.)

After renting around town, the Mu Epsilon Chapter of Beta Theta Pi erected its Tudor Revival house in 1913 on the northeast corner of High and Church Streets. The Raimond Duy Baird Memorial Chapter House, as it is known, displaced the Seth Paddock House, relocated to Home Avenue. This postcard includes a rare view of the original Second Empire–style Seth Butler House to the right, across Church Street. (AM.)

Backyards of houses and fraternities on High Street were once sites of tennis courts and other recreations. Behind Seth Butler's house at the southeast corner of High and Church Streets was a roque court with night lighting. A cross between croquet and billiards, national roque tournaments were played in nearby Norwich. Butler's sons Earle and Dale participated in those games in the 1890s. Earle won the championship in 1896. (MCHS.)

Phi Nu Theta (Eclectic) was Wesleyan's earliest fraternity (1837) and one of the nation's oldest campus fraternal societies. Its new house of 1907 (above) replaced two smaller High Street homes on the east side of the street opposite Cross Street, including one once occupied by Woodrow Wilson. The imposing Neoclassical structure was designed by Henry Bacon and prefigured his masterpiece, the Lincoln Memorial (1914–1922), in Washington. Founded in 1911, Wesleyan's Phi Gamma Chapter of the religious Alpha Chi Rho organization constructed its Colonial Revival house (below) at the northeast corner of High and Court Streets in 1925; Aymar Embury II was the architect. In 1954, the local chapter rebelled against the national fraternity's restriction of membership to Christians only, and by 1959, it evolved as an independent fraternity, Esse Quam Videri, dedicated to diversity in membership. (Above, WULSCA; below, AM.)

ALPHA CHI RHO, WESLEYAN UNIVERSITY
MIDDLETOWN, CONN.

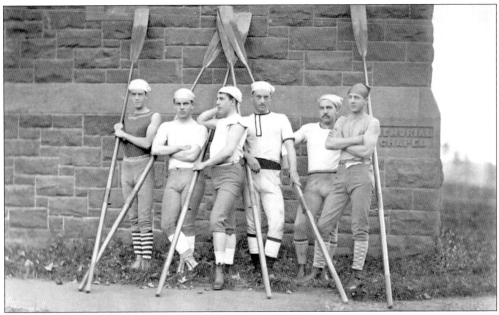

By the 1870s, Brownstone Row buildings became the backdrop for most group photographs. Above, the 1878 rowing club poses at Memorial Chapel. Some pious Methodists believed Wesleyan's sons were corrupted by the metropolitan sport, while students knew the club's success over prestigious schools earned Wesleyan acclaim. The Saratoga Oar trophy, crafted from a victorious Wesleyan oar used there in 1878, is now awarded to the winner of the Little Three Regatta. Below, the class of 1876 poses on the steps of new Judd Hall with musical instruments and paraphernalia representative of their Wesleyan associations. The four females were Wesleyan's first coed graduates: (from left to right) Hannah Ada Taylor, Angie Villette Warren, Phebe Almeda Stone, and Jennie Larned. These early coeds rented rooms in town. In 1883, female students were housed on campus in the First President's House. After 1889, they occupied Webb Hall. (Both, WULSCA.)

These ladies on the rear steps of Webb Hall in 1891 included, from left to right, (first row) Martha Hills, Marie Strobridge, Ellen Peck, and ? Graves; (second row) Lena Adams, Susan-Jane Mantle, ? Graves, Alice Fuller, Christine Glover, Lillian Hart, and Sarah Abbott; (third row) Clara Davis, Vida Moore, Maud Muzzy, Georgia Pottle, Lizzy Rice, and Eva Dilks; (fourth row) Caroline Robbins, Mary O'Flaherty, and ? Latimer, matron of the house. Fear of feminization of Wesleyan led to the end of the generally unpopular coeducation experiment in 1909. While some pushed for a coordinate college for women (proposed for the Samuel C. Hubbard Estate), alumna Elizabeth Wright (class of 1897) led the effort to found in 1915 the Connecticut College for Women in New London. Wesleyan became coed again in 1970. In the meantime, in 1951 (below), returning alumnae posed in solidarity on the steps of the Samuel Russell House. (Both, WULSCA.)

In 1872, Wesleyan president Joseph Cummings, sitting at center on the porch, poses with his faculty on the front steps of the First President's House. Cummings oversaw the expansion of Brownstone Row and introduced coeducation to the campus. In 1862, he was instrumental in starting the Conversational Club, which met for the first time here. The unique group, composed of Wesleyan faculty, administrators, and local citizens, continues to meet to this day. (WULSCA.)

Wesleyan president Willbur Fisk's widow, Ruth Peck Fisk, was given life use of the house at the northwest corner of Cross Street (lower left). She lived here in reclusion until 1885, lovingly cared for by faculty and students who brought her meals, delivered her wood and coal, and ran her errands. The home with the waiting carriage was occupied by Prof. Woodrow Wilson while at Wesleyan (1888–1890). (WULSCA.)

This Italianate house was constructed on the corner of the Hubbard-Pike lot in 1879 by Latin professor Calvin Harrington (Wesleyan class of 1852) and his wife, Eliza. The couple posed with their son Karl (Wesleyan class of 1882), who, like his father, taught Latin at Wesleyan, beginning in 1905. Karl Harrington was also a student of Middletown history, a hymnologist, and an outdoorsman. He lived here until his death in 1953. (Both, AM.)

In 1889, popular literature professor Caleb Winchester constructed his Shingle-style home on the east side of High Street between the E.W.N. Starr House and Delta Kappa Epsilon. "Winch" designed the house with parlor and study at the rear. From these rooms and their rear porch, the Winchesters enjoyed an unparalleled view of the valley. After 1937, it served for many years as Wesleyan's Alumni Guest House. (WULSCA.)

Southward expansion of the Wesleyan campus and the relocation of Cross Street to the south in 1928 disrupted the neighborhood. This College Place house, occupied by many Wesleyan professors, was moved in 1927 to lower Church Street for construction of Shanklin Laboratory. The c. 1835 Greek Revival house of Ferdinand Hart, manufacturer of hoopskirts, was moved to 114 High Street (lower left) about 1919 by the Bailey family, making way for Church Street's extension westward from High Street. The c. 1818 Seth Paddock house had been moved from the northeast corner of High and Church Streets to 34 Home Avenue (lower right) with the construction of the Beta Theta Pi clubhouse in 1913. Rev. Heman Bangs, instrumental in bringing Wesleyan to Middletown, had occupied this house. On Home Avenue, it has been the home of numerous Wesleyan faculty. (Above, WULSCA; below, AM.)

About 1884, Wesleyan classics professor James Van Benschoten remodeled a cottage, constructed about 1839 by Jacob Huber for John Seys, a Methodist missionary to Liberia. "Van Benny," as known by students, Victorianized the cottage with the corner tower, porch, and bay window additions. The house later housed Delta Tau Delta, whose brothers entertained coeds on the front porch. In 1924, it was moved, minus its tower, 200 feet to the south to make way for an addition to Alpha Delta Phi fraternity and is now 167 High Street. Later owners of the David J. Neale House rented it to Omega Phi fraternity, where students shared study space (seen below in 1914). Wesleyan acquired the house in 1924 for use as a men's dormitory. Once covered with ivy, it became known as Ivy Hall and later served the music department. (All, WULSCA.)

The 1875 Charles R.G. Vinal House at the northwest corner of High Street and Wyllis Avenue was acquired by Wesleyan in 1934 and has been the scene of many Wesleyan University functions over the years. Renamed Winchester House until 1996, it first served as alumni office headquarters. Wesleyan graduates returning to campus for Alumni Day in 1948 registered here. The anthropology department later occupied the graceful house. (WULSCA.)

The 11th and longest-serving president of Wesleyan, Victor Butterfield, poses with his wife, Kay, in front of the President's House on High Street in 1966. Butterfield is known for planning post–World War II Wesleyan education and greatly expanding the endowment and physical plant. The university acquired the Coite-Hubbard house from heirs of Jane Miles Hubbard in 1904 to be used as the president's residence. (WULSCA.)

After the Samuel Russell House was obtained by Wesleyan in 1936, it became known as Honors College until 1996. Here, visitors examine senior theses submitted to the honors program in the Thorndike Room at an open house in 1938. Lectures by poets and distinguished authors and Sunday musicales were among the offerings at Honors College. The Russell House is now the home of the philosophy department and an event space. (WULSCA.)

Wesleyan University acquired the T. Macdonough Russell House in 1934 and it became the home of the John Wesley Club in 1954. After the Fisk Hall takeover by African American students in 1969, it was renamed Malcolm X House. These students are meeting around 1975 in the Vanguard Lounge, dedicated to the class of 1969. Now the home of the Center for African American Studies, which achieved full department status on the 50th anniversary of the takeover. (WULSCA.)

Wesleyan acquired the Duane Barnes House from heirs of Louis DeKoven Hubbard in 1934, and through the generosity of George and Harriet Davison, it was converted into the college infirmary. The house was gutted to provide for fireproofing, and an addition was constructed in 1935. Davison was chairman of the university's board of trustees, and the Davison Infirmary was named in memory of the couple's sons Robert and Alfred. Dr. Edgar Fauver was head of the physical education department, athletic director from 1911 to 1937, and university physician from 1913 until his death in 1946. Above, his staff poses with him in 1944. Fauver was an advocate of physical activity and intramural sports but criticized the increasing emphasis on winning in competitive athletics. The antiseptic interior of the health center (below) is an interesting contrast with the gothic exterior of the Barnes House. (Both, WULSCA)

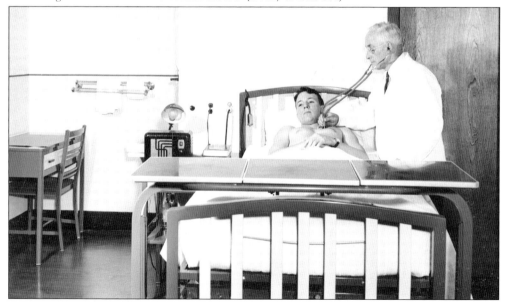

Early-20th-century owners of the 18th-century Whittelsey house, which survived alterations by Charles Alsop and George Hulbert, were Prof. Wilbur Olin Atwater and his wife, Marcia. The couple put their own stamp on the interior with Colonial Revival alterations (right). However, Professor Atwater (Wesleyan class of 1865) spent most of his time at his Judd Hall laboratory where he revolutionized the study of human nutrition with experiments in caloric values. The last private owner, Frank B. Weeks, 64th governor of Connecticut (1909–1911), purchased the home from Marcia Atwater in 1911, months after completing his term. Weeks, a director of the Middletown Mutual Assurance Company and the Middletown Savings Bank, was a delegate to the 1912 Republican National Convention. He bequeathed the home to Wesleyan, and since his death in 1936, the house has served as student housing. (Both, WULSCA.)

In 1936, Wesleyan added a southerly addition to the E.W.N. Starr House (acquired in 1922), and repurposed the old Patten School. Named Downey House after Dr. David G. Downey (Wesleyan class of 1884), past president of the board of trustees, it included a store, post office, and a popular grill room (above). Previously, the Wesleyan Store, post office, and other student offices were in East Hall (below), once known as Webb Hall when coeds lived there. Jailbird singers and a man cranking his "Tin Lizzie" are seen at a class of 1888 reunion. Tragically, East Hall burned down in 1929. Later plans to build a new student center on this site were abandoned in 1973. The Davenport Student Center (formerly Scott Laboratory) served students from 1984 until the Usdan University Center was built on Wyllis Avenue in 2007. (Both, WULSCA.)

FINAL DEVELOPMENT
DOWNEY HOUSE ALTERATIONS
WESLEYAN UNIVERSITY
MIDDLETOWN, CONNECTICUT

Over the years, Wesleyan University proposed building projects for High Street that were either abandoned or modified. Besides the new concrete and glass student center atop the underground power plant across from Brownstone Row that would have significantly changed the street's character, an unexecuted new art museum was also more recently planned to the north of the Richard Alsop IV House. Shreve Lamb & Harmon (architects of the Empire State Building) were engaged by Wesleyan to renovate a few of its acquired houses. They proposed to expand Downey House with a near mirror image of the E.W.N. Starr House to the north (above). Only a portion of the center complex was actually constructed to house the faculty dining room and grill room (below). In 2005, the building was completely renovated for humanities faculty offices and Wesleyan's writing programs. (Both, WULSCA.)

In 1952, Wesleyan acquired the Richard Alsop IV House with funding from George and Harriet Davison. The university built a compatible addition for a new gallery, print room, and vault to house the Davisons' generous bequest of rare prints. After the Alsop family vacated it, the house was rented to Delta Tau Delta fraternity and others, suffering the indignities of the changing tastes of its various tenants (above). Uncovered wall paintings were restored by Wesleyan to their original 1840 appearance (below). Ada Arthur, secretary, descends the stairs while professor of art history Samuel Green, instrumental in the restoration of the house, smokes with an unidentified man in the double parlors that overlooked High Street. The Davison Art Center's collection of prints and photographs has grown to become one of the largest of its kind on any college campus. (Both, WULSCA.)

Five

THEY CAME TO HIGH STREET

Middletown men who made significant contributions to the American Revolution and the new federal government, including Gen. Samuel Holden Parsons, Col. Jabez Hamlin, and Titus Hosmer, who signed the Articles of Confederation, came to worship at High Street's First Church. Pres. John Adams recalled worshiping in First Church in 1771 and called the choir music "the finest singing that I ever heard in my life." Associated with High Street and Wesleyan are four Connecticut (and other state) governors, a Supreme Court justice, many future American presidents, US senators, and countless mayors, legislators, and jurists of distinction.

Acclaimed for its beauty and views over Middletown and the Connecticut River valley, High Street attracted notable visitors throughout its history. When the Marquis de Lafayette toured the town in 1824, horses drew his barouche carriage up Washington and through High Street. Many recorded their impressions of the street. Ralph Waldo Emerson came to speak at Wesleyan in 1845 and wrote to his wife, Lydia, that the "upper street is rich with country palaces."

High Street's private academies and Wesleyan were its greatest draws. Faculty and scholars-in-residence included many preeminent in their fields. Pulitzer Prize winners have taught and studied here. The university also brought to College Row lecturers representing the nation's intellectual and artistic elite. In the 1930s alone, such a diverse group as Robert Frost, Langston Hughes, Walter Lippmann, Margaret Sanger, Reinhold Niebuhr, and LeCorbusier came to speak with students. On her celebrated American tour of 1934–1935, expatriate and writer Gertrude Stein lectured on plays at Wesleyan. Of all the students she met on campuses, Stein admitted that she liked Wesleyan men the best. Alumni of distinction include scientists, doctors, educators, journalists, religious and business leaders, best-selling authors, poets, entertainers, playwrights, movie directors, and Hollywood actors. To name a few would only draw attention to the many not named, so the selections that follow are considered interesting and representative.

This chapter highlights only a few of the fascinating men and women who have been to High Street. Most importantly though, High Street affected the lives of the thousands of students who came "up the hill" from the steamboat landing or the railroad station. Here, they learned from teachers, established longstanding friendships with classmates, and became a part of Middletown's wider community.

Contrary to local legend, Charles Dickens never visited High Street or described it as the most beautiful in America. In 1842, on his American tour, he did recall meeting a woman, "a more beautiful creature I never looked upon." This was Amelia Mather, Samuel Russell's daughter-in-law, who was living on High Street at the time. The confusion started when a reporter wrote, "High Street is a place of wealth, and here, according to Charles Dickens resided the 'Handsomest Girl in America.' " (MCHS.)

On tour in 1859, Edward Everett lectured before 600 Middletown residents. A guest of Samuel and Frances Russell, Everett wrote his wife of their luxurious "palace" and described his host as one of "that set of Americans, who went to China some years ago and made money so fast that they had to provide themselves a barrel and shovel, to shovel in the guineas, they came so fast." (LC.)

High Street was throughout its history always on the route of important city parades and celebrations. As early as 1846, after the agricultural fair concluded in Washington Park, a train of cattle was proudly paraded through the street. High Street residents decorated their houses with lanterns, illuminations, buntings, and billboard transparencies whenever a political or military parade passed by (usually cheered on by Wesleyan's students). This parade in front of the Samuel Russell House (right) was part of Middletown's tercentenary celebration of 1950. The day before, Secretary of State Dean Acheson, who grew up a block from here, visited his hometown to dedicate the new Acheson Drive, the beginning of Route 9 through Middletown. On a more sober note, in 1918 (below), Wesleyan students march in front of Fisk Hall in preparation for World War I. (Right, WULSCA; below, NARA.)

PRES SHANKLIN. STARTING TO MEET PRES TAFT NOV 12TH 1909 MIDDLETOWNCONN.

On November 12, 1909, the city welcomed Pres. William Howard Taft, the first presidential visit since Andrew Jackson in 1832. Taft spoke at the inauguration of Wesleyan president William A. Shanklin. Months were spent planning the welcoming parade of 5,000 down Main Street to the ceremony at the Middlesex Theater and, later, up the hill to campus. Wesleyan's new President's House was decorated with bunting as Shanklin set out in his car to greet Taft that morning. Taft's parade (below) left the Psi Upsilon fraternity house (right), where he had made a brief stop on his way, past Fisk Hall (left), to a luncheon at Shanklin's house. Along with many other dignitaries on that day, Vice Pres. James Sherman attended the daylong events. He was a guest at William W. Wilcox Jr.'s High Street house. (Both, MCHS.)

Two weeks before the national election of 1936, Pres. Franklin Roosevelt was scheduled to motorcade down High Street. Schoolchildren got the day off and, with Wesleyan students, crowded on the hill in front of the Brownstone Row lawn to greet the president. However, last-minute changes rerouted the president's motorcade up Church Street instead. According to claims, Wesleyan students had displayed Alf Landon posters, Communist and Nazi flags were hung from fraternity houses, and it was rumored students might throw firecrackers at the president's car. The disorder was enough to dissuade the Secret Service from the High Street route. Upset adults thronged the street in disbelief (below). Wesleyan's President McConaughy later denied the claims, stating his students "take pride in hospitality, not boorishness." Roosevelt was the most famous person who definitely did not come to High Street. (Both, MCHS.)

Vice Pres. Richard Nixon and his wife, Pat, met with Wesleyan students in front of the two presidents' houses on High Street on a campaign swing through Connecticut on October 18, 1956. That November in Middletown, Nixon and Pres. Dwight Eisenhower received 8,193 votes to 6,077 votes for the Democratic ticket of Adlai Stevenson and Estes Kefauver. Over 60 years later, registered Democrats outnumber Republicans three to one. (WULSCA.)

Sen. Edward Kennedy, scheduled to deliver the May 2008 commencement address at Wesleyan, was diagnosed with a malignant brain tumor the week before. Standing in for him was Sen. Barack Obama, future president of the United States. Obama challenged the graduates to enter public service: "It's only when you hitch your wagon to something larger than yourself that you realize your true potential," he told the commencement audience. (WULSCA.)

In 1832, Charles Bennett Ray (above left) was the first black student to enroll at Wesleyan. Students protested his presence and he was forced to leave after two months. He went on to become a Methodist minister active in the Underground Railroad and, in 1839, became owner and editor of the newspaper *The Colored American*. It was not until 1860 that a black student, Wilbur Fisk Burns (above right), son of a Liberian minister, graduated from Wesleyan. After being denied admission to Wesleyan in 1830, Amos Beman (below), son of Rev. Jehiel Beman of the Cross Street AME Zion Church near the Wesleyan campus, was tutored by Wesleyan student Samuel Dole, until forbidden by the faculty. Beman went on to become a minister and a prominent antislavery and temperance advocate. (Above left, AM; above right, WULSCA; below, BRBML.)

Civil War general George McClellan (right) posed with his close friend Joseph Wright Alsop and railroad paraphernalia. Alsop invested his Middletown family's shipping fortune in railroads and, about 1855, moved into and expanded his cousin Richard Alsop's Italian Villa on High Street. General McClellan, uncomfortable with campaigning, hid from the press and public with the Alsop family in Middletown during his unsuccessful presidential campaign against Abraham Lincoln in 1864. (DAC.)

Babar the Elephant has delighted millions of youngsters since he was conceived by Cecile and Jean de Brunhoff from bedtime stories told to their young sons in Paris. Laurent de Brunhoff continued drawing the children's classic, publishing over 45 books featuring Babar's family, many while living on Wesleyan's campus. Here, Babar the artist imagines himself one of the trompe l'oeil subjects at the Richard Alsop IV House on High Street. (WULSCA.)

Peter Morse Hunting (Wesleyan class of 1963) was raised in Connecticut and the Midwest and walked High Street, as did his colonial ancestors the Russells and Huntingtons. Here, he sits with his fraternity brothers on the front porch of the Alpha Delta Phi house around 1963. From left to right are Bill Owens, Gus Lemesis, Jim Russell, Mike Timm (upside down), Mike Michalczyk (standing), Dave Kevis, Pete Hunting (arms crossed over chest), Bob Hirschfeld, and Steve Lockwood. Pete's altruism led him to Vietnam, where he worked with farmers, teachers, and youth. As an International Voluntary Services noncombatant, he designed and built windmills around 1964. He met an untimely death at the hands of the Viet Cong on November 12, 1965, the first civilian aid worker and Wesleyan graduate to die in Vietnam. (Both, courtesy of Jill Hunting.)

Rev. Dr. Martin Luther King Jr. spent the summer of 1944 picking tobacco in Connecticut; this experience of escaping the Jim Crow–era South changed the trajectory of his life. On June 7, 1964, he delivered the baccalaureate address at Wesleyan University and is pictured at right leaving Memorial Chapel with president emeritus Victor Butterfield (left) and associate professor of religion and fellow freedom rider John Maguire (behind King). (WULSCA.)

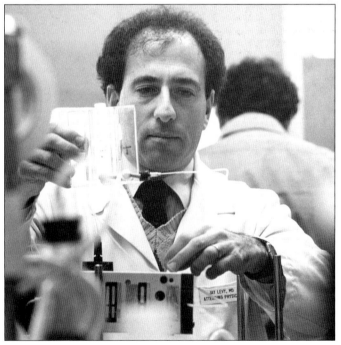

Dr. Jay Levy graduated from Wesleyan with high honors in 1960, received his medical degree from Columbia University, and embarked on a career devoted to researching the cause of viral diseases. He began researching AIDS in 1981 and discovered the AIDS virus, HIV, in 1983. After writing a college paper on the play *Waiting for Godot*, Levy began a lifelong friendship with its author, Nobel Prize–winner Samuel Beckett. (WULSCA.)

Running legends Bill Rodgers (Wesleyan class of 1970), third from left, and Ambrose "Amby" Burfoot (Wesleyan class of 1968), second from right, honed their skills on the university's cross-country team. Rodgers went on to win both the Boston and New York Marathons four times each. Amby, Bill's college roommate, won the Boston Marathon in 1968 while still a student. He was the editor-in-chief of *Runner's World* magazine for many years. (WULSCA.)

Born in Kibera, a slum in Nairobi, Kenya, Kennedy Odede had dreams of improving the lives of Kibera's residents. Jessica Posner (Wesleyan class of 2009), a study abroad student from Wesleyan who volunteered in Kibera, encouraged him to join her at Wesleyan, and he delivered the student address at his graduation in 2012. Now married, they founded Shining Hope for Communities, which provides education for girls and related services in Kibera. (SHOFCO.)

The Highwaymen were a folk group formed by Wesleyan University freshmen (from left to right) Dave Fisher, Bob Burnett, Steve Butts, Chan Daniels, and Steve Trott in 1958. In September 1961, their rendition of the old African American work song, which they titled "Michael (Row the Boat Ashore)," hit No. 1 on the US *Billboard* Hot 100 Chart. The members of the group went on to successful careers in music, law, and business. (WULSCA.)

Lin-Manuel Miranda, composer, lyricist, and original star of the Tony-winning musicals *In The Heights* and *Hamilton*, graduated with the Wesleyan class of 2002. Here, he celebrates in front of Memorial Chapel with, from left to right, his sister Luz Miranda-Crespo; mother, Dr. Luz Towns-Miranda; and father, Luis A. Miranda Jr. (Courtesy of the Miranda family.)

New York–based architect Henry Bacon left his mark on High Street and Wesleyan University with his master plan of 1913. But he also designed Olin Library (with McKim, Mead & White), Eclectic (1907), Skull & Serpent Society (1914), Clark Hall (1916), Van Vleck Observatory (1916), and South College's belfry (1916), as well as remodeling many campus buildings, before designing the Lincoln Memorial in Washington, DC, for which he is remembered. (LC.)

Nancy Nash Campbell, wife of Wesleyan president Colin Campbell, took particular interest in High Street's architecture, founding the Wesleyan Landmarks Advisory Board in 1973, which advised Wesleyan on matters relating to its historic properties. She went on to chair the National Trust for Historic Preservation and the Montpelier Foundation, overseeing US president James Madison's home. She is the recipient of numerous historic preservation awards and an honorary doctorate from Wesleyan. (CWF/HU.)

Index of Buildings

Index of Buildings by Street Address

DISCOVER THOUSANDS OF LOCAL HISTORY BOOKS FEATURING MILLIONS OF VINTAGE IMAGES

Arcadia Publishing, the leading local history publisher in the United States, is committed to making history accessible and meaningful through publishing books that celebrate and preserve the heritage of America's people and places.

Find more books like this at
www.arcadiapublishing.com

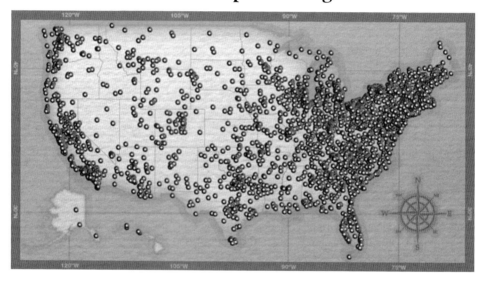

Search for your hometown history, your old stomping grounds, and even your favorite sports team.

Consistent with our mission to preserve history on a local level, this book was printed in South Carolina on American-made paper and manufactured entirely in the United States. Products carrying the accredited Forest Stewardship Council (FSC) label are printed on 100 percent FSC-certified paper.

MADE IN THE